The Basic Elements of Music

By:
Catherine Schmidt-Jones

The Basic Elements of Music

By:
Catherine Schmidt-Jones

Online:
<http://cnx.org/content/col10218/1.7/ >

CONNEXIONS

Rice University, Houston, Texas

©2008 Catherine Schmidt-Jones

This selection and arrangement of content is licensed under the Creative Commons Attribution License:
http://creativecommons.org/licenses/by/1.0

Table of Contents

1 Time Elements
  1.1 Rhythm 1
  1.2 Simple Rhythm Activities 2
  1.3 Meter in Music 5
  1.4 Musical Meter Activities 7
  1.5 Tempo 12
  1.6 A Tempo Activity 15
  1.7 Dynamics and Accents in Music 16
  1.8 A Musical Dynamics Activity 19
  1.9 A Musical Accent Activity 21
  Solutions 25

2 Pitch Elements
  2.1 Timbre 27
  2.2 Melody 32
  2.3 Harmony 52
  Solutions .... ??

3 Combining Time and Pitch
  3.1 The Textures of Music 65
  3.2 A Musical Textures Activity 67
  3.3 An Introduction to Counterpoint 71
  3.4 Counterpoint Activities 73
  3.5 Form in Music 79
  3.6 Music Form Activities 83
  Solutions 87

Index 88
Attributions 91

Chapter 1

Time Elements

1.1 Rhythm[1]

Rhythm, melody (Section 2.2.1), harmony (Section 2.3.1), timbre (Section 2.1.1), and texture (Section 3.1) are the essential aspects of a musical performance. They are often called the basic elements of music. The main purpose of music theory is to describe various pieces of music in terms of their similarities and differences in these elements, and music is usually grouped into genres based on similarities in all or most elements. It's useful, therefore, to be familiar with the terms commonly used to describe each element. Because harmony is the most highly developed aspect of Western music[2], music theory tends to focus almost exclusively on melody and harmony. Music does not have to have harmony, however, and some music doesn't even have melody. So perhaps the other three elements can be considered the most basic components of music.

Music cannot happen without time. The placement of the sounds in time is the rhythm of a piece of music. Because music must be heard over a period of time, rhythm is one of the most basic elements of music. In some pieces of music, the rhythm is simply a "placement in time" that cannot be assigned a beat[3] or meter (Section 1.3), but most rhythm terms concern more familiar types of music with a steady beat. See Meter (Section 1.3) for more on how such music is organized, and Duration[4] and Time Signature[5] for more on how to read and write rhythms. See Simple Rhythm Activities (Section 1.2) for easy ways to encourage children to explore rhythm.

Rhythm Terms

- **Rhythm** - The term "rhythm" has more than one meaning. It can mean the basic, repetitive pulse of the music, or a rhythmic pattern that is repeated throughout the music (as in "feel the rhythm"). It can also refer to the pattern in time of a single small group of notes (as in "play this rhythm for me").
- **Beat** - Beat also has more than one meaning, but always refers to music with a steady pulse. It may refer to the pulse itself (as in "play this note on beat two of the measure[6]"). **On the beat** or **on the downbeat** refer to the moment when the pulse is strongest. **Off the beat** is in between pulses, and the **upbeat** is exactly halfway between pulses. **Beat** may also refer to a specific repetitive rhythmic pattern that maintains the pulse (as in "it has a Latin beat"). Note that once a strong feeling of having a beat is established, it is not necessary for something to happen on every beat; a beat can still be "felt" even if it is not specifically heard.
- **Measure or bar** - Beats are grouped into measures or bars. The first beat is usually the strongest, and in most music, most of the bars have the same number of beats. This sets up an underlying

---

[1]This content is available online at <http://cnx.org/content/m11646/1.4/>.
[2]"What Kind of Music is That?" <http://cnx.org/content/m11421/latest/>
[3]"Time Signature": Section Beats and Measures <http://cnx.org/content/m10956/latest/#s1>
[4]"Duration: Note Lengths in Written Music" <http://cnx.org/content/m10945/latest/>
[5]"Time Signature" <http://cnx.org/content/m10956/latest/>
[6]"Time Signature": Section Beats and Measures <http://cnx.org/content/m10956/latest/#s1>

pattern in the pulse of the music: for example, strong-weak-strong-weak-strong-weak, or strong-weak-weak-strong-weak-weak. (See Meter (Section 1.3).)
- **Rhythm Section** - The rhythm section of a band is the group of instruments that usually provide the background rhythm and chords. The rhythm section almost always includes a percussionist (usually on a drum set) and a bass player (usually playing a plucked string bass of some kind). It may also include a piano and/or other keyboard players, more percussionists, and one or more guitar players or other strummed or plucked strings. Vocalists, wind instruments, and bowed strings are usually not part of the rhythm section.
- **Syncopation** - Syncopation occurs when a strong note happens either on a weak beat or off the beat. See Syncopation[7].

1.2 Simple Rhythm Activities[8]

Here are three simple classroom activities that promote accuracy in two areas (rhythms and keeping time) that are fundamental for good musical performance: Rhythm Imitations (Section 1.2.1: Activity 1: Rhythm Imitations), Karaoke Percussion (Section 1.2.2: Activity 2: Karaoke Percussion), and No Karaoke Percussion (Section 1.2.3: Activity 3: No Karaoke Percussion). The activities can also be used to develop awareness of the effect of percussion and rhythm on musical styles.

Goals and Standards

- **Grade Level** - K-12 (adaptable for a wide range of ages and musical experience)
- **Student Prerequisites** - Any student who can clap along with a steady beat is ready for these activities. The activities will still have value for older students with more musical experience if the rhythms are sufficiently complex and/or a discussion of musical styles is included.
- **Teacher Expertise** - Teacher training in music education is not necessary to present this activity, but the teacher should be capable of presenting rhythms accurately and consistently. (See Rhythm (Section 1.1) and Meter (Section 1.3).)
- **Music Standards Addressed** - National Standards for Music Education[9] standard 2 (performing on instruments, alone and with others, a varied repertoire of music). If the Karaoke activities include a discussion of percussion backgrounds as an element of style, this also addresses music standards 6 (listening to, analyzing, and describing music) and 9 (understanding music in relation to history and culture). If the students are reading written rhythms, standard 5 (reading and notating music) is also addressed.
- **Evaluation** - For assessment, decide on a level of rhythmic complexity that the student should be able to achieve in echoing rhythms or in playing a consistent, independent percussion part, then assess whether the student is succeeding at that level. If not, these activities may be repeated throughout the school year, with gradual increases in complexity as the students get more practice.
- **Follow-up** - Help develop basic rhythmic skills in the students by continuing to give them, throughout the school year, simple rhythm parts to accompany music they are learning, and continuing to ask them to echo specific rhythms, particularly rhythms that they are learning to read or perform.

1.2.1 Activity 1: Rhythm Imitations

Objectives

- **Time Requirements** - This activity works best as a short (5-15 minute) class warm-up done often in preparation for other musical activities (such as singing, playing instruments, or doing the activities below).

---
[7]"Syncopation" <http://cnx.org/content/m11644/latest/>
[8]This content is available online at <http://cnx.org/content/m14258/1.6/>.
[9]http://menc.org/resources/view/national-standards-for-music-education

- **Objectives** - The student will perform specific rhythms accurately, either while reading them or immediately after hearing them.

Materials and Preparation

- No preparation is necessary if you want the students to copy heard rhythms.
- If you want the students to read written rhythms, write some short rhythmic figures, beginning with very simple rhythms and gradually adding complexity, or find some music with rhythms of the appropriate complexity. Any single-line music will do for this; students should be encouraged to be capable of ignoring the melodic information, when asked to convey only the rhythmic information in the line.

Procedure

- Clap (or play on a rhythm instrument) any short rhythm (or, for students learning to read music, have the student read a written rhythm).
- Have a student clap or play the same rhythm back to you, at the same speed.
- For students who find this challenging (or if you have difficulty deciding whether or not they echoed your rhythm correctly), keep the rhythms short and simple. For students who do well, give them longer, more challenging rhythms to echo.

Variations

1. Make the rhythm a collection of claps, stomps, and other sounds. (Keep it short unless the students are quite good at it.) Have the student copy it using the correct sounds.
2. Make the rhythm a collection of sounds on any percussion instruments you have available. (See Percussion Fast and Cheap[10] for suggestions.)
3. Make this a game, with students taking turns imitating your rhythm (change it often). Students have to sit down if they miss a rhythm, and the last student standing wins.
4. Let the students have their turn making up short rhythms for each other to imitate.
5. If you don't have very many students, you can make this a game in which each student gets more and more difficult rhythms until they miss one. Keep track of how many each student got correct before they missed.
6. If you want the students to echo the rhythms as a group rather than individually, you will probably need to "count off" for them. Count 2 or 4 beats before you start your rhythm, and then give them exactly the same count to start theirs.

1.2.2 Activity 2: Karaoke Percussion

Objectives

- **Time Requirements** - Allow one (approximately 45-minute) class period if it will take the students some time to learn their rhythms. If the students can learn the rhythms very quickly, this activity can be done as a 5-15-minute warm-up before other music activities, or as an active break between desk-work sessions.
- **Objectives** - The student will perform a rhythmic ostinato (suitable to the student's age and musical experience) as an accompaniment to a recording, keeping an accurate rhythm and beat.

Materials and Preparation

- Be prepared for a noisy activity.

---

[10]"Percussion Fast and Cheap" <http://cnx.org/content/m11889/latest/>

- Have percussion instruments ready for the class to use or have the class make their own instruments ahead of time. (See Percussion Fast and Cheap[11].) Don't forget the possibilities of "found percussion" (pots, lids, spoons, pencils, books, etc.) and "body percussion" (claps, slaps, finger snaps, stomps, etc.).
- Select music that you will be adding karaoke percussion to. Cheerful, fast-tempo music that your students enjoy is best. If you are going to include a discussion of percussion as an element of style, make sure you include music from a variety of styles (for example, various kinds of pop, rock, jazz, and world music). Have your tape or CD player ready, and have tapes ready at the correct spot or know CD track numbers.
- Unless you will have the students invent the rhythms to be played, you may want to decide on them ahead of time. Use rhythms of appropriate complexity: for beginners, this may be simply playing on the beat, playing off the beat (harder!), playing only on alternate beats or only on the first or last beat of a measure; experienced students will want something more complex and interesting.

Procedure
- Usually you add the vocal parts when doing karaoke, but in this activity, the class is going to add percussion parts. For very young children, this will probably mean simply adding noise. That is fine, although you can encourage them to add the noise on the beat or only during certain phrases in the music.
- Encourage older students to add a particular repetitive rhythm to the music. Beginners may all need to be on the same rhythm. More musically experienced students may each be given a different rhythm.
- Have the students listen to the song first. Have them clap along, so that they feel the basic beat of the music. Children with some musical experience may be able to identify rhythms that are already being emphasized in the music. Encourage older, musically experienced students to come up with a steady, patterned rhythm that fits the music. For other students, teach them the rhythms that you have decided on, by letting them play each rhythm with you.
- As much as possible, students should play different, complementary rhythms, instead of all playing the same rhythm. This activity is most fun for small groups, with each student having a different instrument and rhythm so that everybody is contributing a unique sound. Break a larger class into small groups of students learning (or agreeing on and practicing) the same rhythm on the same type of instrument. If possible, break the class into smaller performing groups (with one student from each rhythm group) once the rhythms are learned, and allow the groups to perform for each other, giving each student a chance to play their rhythm independently.
- Let the students experiment and settle on their rhythms with the music playing, then have a "performance" with everybody doing their chosen rhythms. This is even more effective if students enter one at a time (you can point to a student when it is her turn to enter) and then steadily continue their chosen rhythm as more students enter.
- Students with some musical sophistication will enjoy the challenge of adding percussion in a "stylistically appropriate" way. Work with the students to come up with "percussion tracks" for several pieces in very different styles. Discuss differences in choice of instruments and in rhythms for the different styles.

1.2.3 Activity 3: No Karaoke Percussion

- **Time Requirements** - If it will take some time to teach all the students their parts, allow one (approximately 45-minute) class period. If the students will learn and perform their rhythms quickly, use this as a 5-15-minute class warm-up before other music activities, or as an active break between desk-work sessions.
- **Objectives** - The student will perform a rhythmic ostinato that complements other rhythmic ostinatos being performed simultaneously, keeping accurate rhythm and a steady beat.

---

[11]"Percussion Fast and Cheap" <http://cnx.org/content/m11889/latest/>

- **Extension** - Musically experienced students who succeed at this activity can be asked to provide both percussion and vocal parts for a song, with no recorded support. (You may want to provide piano or other accompaniment.) Have the students decide on a variety of rhythmic ostinatos to accompany a song that they know well. Have them sing and play the rhythm parts at the same time.

Materials and Preparation

- If your students have a strong sense of rhythm, they can do this no-background-music version of the activity.
- Provide each student with a percussion instrument, or let them decide on their own "found" or "body" percussion.
- Decide whether you will provide and teach the rhythms, or let the students come up with their own, or use the same rhythms they have been playing in the previous activity.

Procedure

- Designate one student with a fairly loud instrument as the beat keeper. This student establishes the beat and plays steadily on the beat during the entire session.
- Other students enter one at a time, steadily playing their rhythms, to produce a complex rhythmic ostinato. If they do this well, the result should sound like the background rhythm track to a pop, rock, or Latin tune.
- Once all students have been playing for some time, the beat keeper can end the session. Or, for more of a challenge, the beat keeper can name a student, who must then play a different rhythm.
- For students ready for a challenge, teach them, or ask them to come up with, several very different "percussion tracks" (using different instruments and different rhythms and meters). After playing each ostinato for some time, ask the students what style or genre of music it might be used for. Can they identify the elements (instruments? a particular rhythm? meter?) that most strongly suggests that style or genre?

1.2.4 Other Rhythm Activities Available

You can find other activities that explore various aspects of rhythm in Music Conducting: Classroom Activities[12], A Tempo Activity (Section 1.6), Musical Meter Activities (Section 1.4), Talking Drums[13], and Message Drums[14]. For more about reading rhythms, see Duration: Note Length[15], Duration: Rest Lengths[16] and Time Signature[17].

1.3 Meter in Music[18]

1.3.1 What is Meter?

The **meter** of a piece of music is the arrangment of its rhythms in a repetitive pattern of strong and weak beats. This does not necessarily mean that the rhythms themselves are repetitive, but they do strongly suggest a repeated pattern of pulses. It is on these pulses, the beat[19] of the music, that you tap your foot, clap your hands, dance, etc.

---

[12]"Music Conducting: Classroom Activities" <http://cnx.org/content/m11031/latest/>
[13]"Talking Drums" <http://cnx.org/content/m11872/latest/>
[14]"Message Drums" <http://cnx.org/content/m11422/latest/>
[15]"Duration: Note Lengths in Written Music" <http://cnx.org/content/m10945/latest/>
[16]"Duration: Rest Length" <http://cnx.org/content/m11887/latest/>
[17]"Time Signature" <http://cnx.org/content/m10956/latest/>
[18]This content is available online at <http://cnx.org/content/m12405/1.7/>.
[19]"Time Signature": Section Beats and Measures <http://cnx.org/content/m10956/latest/#s1>

Some music does not have a meter. Ancient music, such as Gregorian chants; new music, such as some experimental twentieth-century art music; and Non-Western music, such as some native American flute music, may not have a strong, repetitive pattern of beats. Other types of music, such as traditional Western African drumming, may have very complex meters that can be difficult for the beginner to identify.

But most Western[20] music has simple, repetitive patterns of beats. This makes **meter** a very useful way to organize the music. Common notation[21], for example, divides the written music into small groups of beats called measures, or bars[22]. The lines dividing each measure from the next help the musician reading the music to keep track of the rhythms (Section 1.1). A piece (or section of the piece) is assigned a time signature[23] that tells the performer how many beats to expect in each measure, and what type of note[24] should get one beat. (For more on reading time signatures, please see Time Signature[25].)

Conducting[26] also depends on the meter of the piece; conductors use different conducting patterns for the different meters. These patterns emphasize the differences between the stronger and weaker beats to help the performers keep track of where they are in the music.

But the conducting patterns depend only on the pattern of strong and weak beats. In other words, they only depend on "how many beats there are in a measure", not "what type of note gets a beat". So even though the time signature is often called the "meter" of a piece, one can talk about meter without worrying about the time signature or even being able to read music. (Teachers, note that this means that children can be introduced to the concept of meter long before they are reading music. See Meter Activities (Section 1.4) for some suggestions.)

1.3.2 Classifying Meters

Meters can be classified by counting the number of beats from one strong beat to the next. For example, if the meter of the music feels like "strong-weak-strong-weak", it is in **duple** meter. "strong-weak-weak-strong-weak-weak" is **triple** meter, and "strong-weak-weak-weak" is **quadruple**. (Most people don't bother classifying the more unusual meters, such as those with five beats in a measure.)

Meters can also be classified as either simple or compound. In a **simple** meter, each beat is basically divided into halves. In **compound** meters, each beat is divided into thirds.

A **borrowed division** occurs whenever the basic meter of a piece is interrupted by some beats that sound like they are "borrowed" from a different meter. One of the most common examples of this is the use of triplets[27] to add some compound meter to a piece that is mostly in a simple meter. (See Dots, Ties, and Borrowed Divisions[28] to see what borrowed divisions look like in common notation.)

1.3.3 Recognizing Meters

To learn to recognize meter, remember that (in most Western[29] music) the beats and the subdivisions of beats are all equal and even. So you are basically listening for a running, even pulse underlying the rhythms of the music. For example, if it makes sense to count along with the music "ONE-and-Two-and-ONE-and-Two-and" (with all the syllables very evenly spaced) then you probably have a simple duple meter. But if it's more comfortable to count "ONE-and-a-Two-and-a-ONE-and-a-Two-and-a", it's probably compound duple meter. (Make sure numbers always come on a pulse, and "one" always on the strongest pulse.)

This may take some practice if you're not used to it, but it can be useful practice for anyone who is learning about music. To help you get started, the figure below sums up the most-used meters. To help give

---

[20]"What Kind of Music is That?" <http://cnx.org/content/m11421/latest/>
[21]"The Staff" <http://cnx.org/content/m10880/latest/>
[22]"Time Signature": Section Beats and Measures <http://cnx.org/content/m10956/latest/#s1>
[23]"Time Signature" <http://cnx.org/content/m10956/latest/>
[24]"Duration: Note Lengths in Written Music" <http://cnx.org/content/m10945/latest/>
[25]"Time Signature" <http://cnx.org/content/m10956/latest/>
[26]"Conducting" <http://cnx.org/content/m12404/latest/>
[27]"Dots, Ties, and Borrowed Divisions" <http://cnx.org/content/m11888/latest/#p3d>
[28]"Dots, Ties, and Borrowed Divisions" <http://cnx.org/content/m11888/latest/>
[29]"What Kind of Music is That?" <http://cnx.org/content/m11421/latest/>

you an idea of what each meter should feel like, here are some animations (with sound) of duple simple[30], duple compound[31], triple simple[32], triple compound[33], quadruple simple[34], and quadruple compound[35] meters. You may also want to listen to some examples of music that is in simple duple[36], simple triple[37], simple quadruple[38], compound duple[39], and compound triple[40] meters.

Meters

Meter	Count											Example Time Signature
Duple Simple	1	&	2	&								2/4
Triple Simple	1	&	2	&	3	&						3/4
Quadruple Simple	1	&	2	&	3	&	4	&				4/4
Duple Compound	1	&	a	2	&	a						6/8
Triple Compound	1	&	a	2	&	a	3	&	a			9/8
Quadruple Compound	1	&	a	2	&	a	3	&	a	4	& a	12/8

Figure 1.1: Remember that meter is not the same as time signature; the time signatures given here are just examples. For example, 2/2 and 2/8 are also simple duple meters.

1.4 Musical Meter Activities[41]

1.4.1 Introduction

Children do not have to learn to read music in order to recognize meter. In fact, a child who is already comfortable with the concept (and feel) of meter may have less trouble learning to read music, follow a conductor[42], and understand written notes[43] and time signatures[44]. For definitions and other information on meter, please see Meter in Music (Section 1.3). The activities below include Listen for Meter (Section 1.4.2: Listen for Meter), Sing with Meter (Section 1.4.3: Sing with Meter), Dance with Meter (Section 1.4.4: Dance with Meter), and Recognize Meter in Time Signature (Section 1.4.5: Recognize Meter in Time Signatures)

---

[30] http://cnx.org/content/m12405/latest/duplesimple.swf
[31] http://cnx.org/content/m12405/latest/duplecompound.swf
[32] http://cnx.org/content/m12405/latest/triplesimple.swf
[33] http://cnx.org/content/m12405/latest/triplecompound.swf
[34] http://cnx.org/content/m12405/latest/quadsimple.swf
[35] http://cnx.org/content/m12405/latest/quadcompound.swf
[36] http://cnx.org/content/m12405/latest/metdup.mp3
[37] http://cnx.org/content/m12405/latest/mettrip.mp3
[38] http://cnx.org/content/m12405/latest/metquad.mp3
[39] http://cnx.org/content/m12405/latest/metcompdup.mp3
[40] http://cnx.org/content/m12405/latest/metcomptrip.mp3
[41] This content is available online at <http://cnx.org/content/m13616/1.5/>.
[42] "Conducting" <http://cnx.org/content/m12404/latest/>
[43] "Duration: Note Lengths in Written Music" <http://cnx.org/content/m10945/latest/>
[44] "Time Signature" <http://cnx.org/content/m10956/latest/>

Goals and Assessment

- **Goals** - The student will recognize specific meters in aural examples of music, and will demonstrate meter actively by appropriate clapping, vocalization, and/or movement, or by identifying a likely time signature.
- **Music Standards Addressed** - National Standards for Music Education[45] standard 6 (listening to, analyzing, and describing music), and (for Recognize Meter in Time Signature (Section 1.4.5: Recognize Meter in Time Signatures) only) 5 (reading and notating music).
- **Other Subjects Addressed** - The activity also addresses National Dance Standards[46] standard 1 (identifying and demonstrating movement elements and skills in performing dance), 2 (understanding the choreographic principles, processes, and structures)

1.4.2 Listen for Meter

Objectives and Assessment

- **Grade Level** - preK (if developmentally ready) - 12
- **Student Prerequisites** - Students should be able to accurately identify and clap along with the beat of a piece of music.
- **Teacher Expertise** - The teacher should be familiar and comfortable with the terms and concepts regarding meter (Section 1.3), and should be able to accurately and easily identify heard meter.
- **Time Requirements** - If you have many different musical examples, and will also be exploring simple and compound meters, this activity may take one (approximately 45-minute) class period. It may also be done as a short (5-15-minute) warm-up to other music activities or as a break from desk work.
- **Objectives** - Given an aural example of music, the student will clap to the beat, distinguish weak from strong beats, and clap only on strong beats. The student will identify the meter of the music by determining the number of weak beats for every strong beat.
- **Extensions** - Advanced students may be asked to distinguish heard beat subdivisions by vocalizing with them, and to identify whether the meter is simple or compound. For students who are learning to read music, see Recognize Meter in Time Signatures (Section 1.4.5: Recognize Meter in Time Signatures).
- **Evaluation** - During the activity, assess whether each student can do the following independently (without waiting to imitate the teacher or other students), along with others, in direct imitation of others, or not at all: clap on the beat, clap only on the strong beats, count the number of weak beats for each strong beat, vocalize with the beat subdivisions, and name the meter. If students are not at the level you would like, repeat the activity occasionally throughout the year.
- **Follow-up** - Help commit these lessons to long-term memory, by continuing throughout the year to ask students to identify the meter of music that they are hearing or learning.

Materials and Preparation

- You will need some tapes or CDs of songs the students will enjoy, with a good mix of different meters. Choose songs with strong beats and simple tunes, songs in which the meter is very obvious to you. You may want to choose one or two tricky examples to save for the end if the students are doing well.
- You will need an audio player to play the songs for the class. Have the tapes ready to play at your chosen selection, or know the CD track numbers.

Procedure

1. First, explain duple, triple, and quadruple meters (see Meter in Music (p. 6)).

---

[45] http://menc.org/resources/view/national-standards-for-music-education
[46] http://www.pecentral.org/lessonideas/dance/dancestandards.html

2. Have the children listen to a song. Encourage them at first to tap their toes on all of the beats. Then ask them to clap only on the strong beats and/or to count 1-2-1-2-, or 1-2-3-1-2-3- or 1-2-3-4-
3. Ask them to decide as a group, based on their clapping or counting, the meter of the song. Don't be surprised if they can't agree on whether a piece is duple or quadruple; these are sometimes hard to distinguish. In fact, two trained musicians may disagree as to whether a piece "feels" as if it is in 2 or 4.
4. If they do well with the above steps on several songs, explain the difference between simple and compound meters. (See Meter in Music (p. 6). You may want to copy the figure in that lesson as a visual aid for them, or have them watch and/or listen to the animations.)
5. You can use the same songs they've already heard or try new ones. Once they've found the beat, have them try chanting along with the music "one-and-two-and-", or "one-and-a-two-and-a-" (for duple meters). If the music is fast, and "one-and-a" is too difficult, you can switch to easy-to-say nonsense syllables, for example "doodle" for simple and "doodle-uh" for compound. If you are using a particular music method, use the syllables favored by that method.
6. Can they decide which falls more naturally with the music? Is the meter simple or compound? Do they hear clues in the melody or the percussion or the bass line that help them decide?

1.4.3 Sing with Meter

Objectives and Assessment

- **Grade Level** - preK (if developmentally ready) - 12
- **Student Prerequisites** - Students should be able to accurately identify and clap along with the beat of a piece of music while they are singing it.
- **Teacher Expertise** - The teacher should be familiar and comfortable with the terms and concepts regarding meter (Section 1.3), , should be able to accurately and easily identify meter, and should be comfortable leading the singing.
- **Time Requirements** - If you have plenty of songs, and will also be exploring simple and compound meters, this activity may take one (approximately 45-minute) class period. It may also be done as a short (5-15-minute) warm-up to other music activities or as a break from desk work, or you may do both Listen for Meter (Section 1.4.2: Listen for Meter) and "Sing with Meter" in one class period.
- **Objectives** - While singing, the student will clap to the beat, distinguish weak from strong beats, and clap only on strong beats. The student will identify the meter of the music by determining the number of weak beats for every strong beat.
- **Extensions** - Advanced students may be asked to distinguish heard beat subdivisions by vocalizing with them, and to identify whether the meter is simple or compound. For students who are learning to read music, see Recognize Meter in Time Signatures (Section 1.4.5: Recognize Meter in Time Signatures).
- **Evaluation** - During the activity, assess whether each student can do the following independently (without waiting to imitate the teacher or other students), along with others, in imitation of others, or not at all: while singing, clap on the beat, clap only on the strong beats; while listening to others sing, count the number of weak beats for each strong beat, vocalize with the beat subdivisions, and name the meter. If students are not at the level you would like, repeat the activity occasionally throughout the year.
- **Follow-up** - Help commit these lessons to long-term memory, by continuing throughout the year to ask students to identify the meter of music that they are singing.

Materials and Preparation

- You won't need any audio equipment for this one, but if you play piano (or guitar), you may want to choose songs you can accompany.

- Again, choose songs with a variety of meters. Some students will find singing and clapping at the same time to be more of a challenge; choose simple songs that the children already know how to sing confidently, with a steady, consistent beat and strong rhythm. Songs that they are already learning in music class are an excellent choice.

Procedure

1. The procedure is similar to the "Listen for Meter" procedure. This time, the children will tap their toes and clap while they are singing.
2. When listening for simple or compound meter, let the students take turns; some will sing while others are counting the beats and divisions of beats. If the melody is very simple, older students with more musical experience may be able to sing "one-and-two-and-etc.", to the tune, but remember that the rhythm of the song is not the same as the meter, and the two will not always match up, even in a simple song.

Suggested Simple Songs to Sing

- "Yankee Doodle" (duple simple)
- "London Bridge" (duple simple)
- "Row, Row, Row Your Boat" (duple compound)
- "Three Blind Mice" (duple compound)
- "Did You Ever See a Lassie" (triple simple)
- "Home on the Range" (triple simple)
- "Clementine" (triple; some people give this folk song a simple meter straight-eighth-note feel; others give it a swing[47], compound feel)
- "Amazing Grace" (triple; again, some people sing "straight" simple meter; others sing "swing" compound meter)
- "Frere Jaque" (quadruple simple)
- "America the Beautiful" (quadruple simple)
- "I've Been Working on the Railroad" (quadruple; simple or compound, depending on how you sing it)

1.4.4 Dance with Meter

Objectives and Assessment

- **Grade Level** - preK (if developmentally ready) - 12
- **Student Prerequisites** - Students should be able to accurately identify and move to the beat of heard music.
- **Teacher Expertise** - The teacher should be familiar and comfortable with the terms and concepts regarding meter (Section 1.3), should be able to accurately and easily identify heard meter, and should be comfortable leading the choreographed movements with the beat.
- **Time Requirements** - If you have plenty of music, this activity may take one (approximately 45-minute) class period. It may also be done as a short (5-15-minute) warm-up to other music activities or as a break from desk work, or you may do it with Listen for Meter (Section 1.4.2: Listen for Meter) or Sing with Meter (Section 1.4.3: Sing with Meter) to fill one class period.
- **Objectives** - The student will learn a simple, repetitive choreography that reflects the meter of the music, and perform it accurately and on the beat.
- **Extensions** - Advanced students may be asked to design a set of movements that works well with the meter.
- **Evaluation** - During the activity, assess whether each student is learning the movements correctly and moving with the beat and meter.

---

[47]"Dots, Ties, and Borrowed Divisions" <http://cnx.org/content/m11888/latest/#p3e>

Materials and Preparation

- Do at least one of the other meter activities above before this one, so that the students are familiar with the concept.
- Find music with a variety of (steady) meters and tempos (Section 1.5) that the students will enjoy moving to.
- Bring tapes or CDs of the music and an audio player to class. Have the tapes ready to play your selections, or know the track numbers for CD selections.
- Before the activity begins, you may want to work out at least one sample choreography for each meter. Depending on the students' abilities, this can be as simple as marching (left-right-left-right) to a duple meter, or something much more involved. Reserving steps, hops, turns, and other weight-shifting movements for strong beats is best. Make sure you always do the same thing on the same beat: step forward on one, back on two, for example. Kicks, foot slides and shuffles, are fine for weaker beats. Try using claps, finger snaps, and other things that don't involve shifting the entire body, for the "and" and "and-a" upbeats.

Procedure

1. You may have the students decide the meter of each piece (see activities above), or simply tell them. The point of this activity is to "act out" the meter physically.
2. Teach the students your choreography, pointing out how it fits the meter of the music.
3. Let them "dance" to the music.
4. Try a different piece with a different meter or tempo (Section 1.5) and different choreography.
5. As the students get the idea, encourage them to come up with motions to be incorporated into the new choreography. You may let the students design the entire choreography themselves, but make sure that it "fits" the meter.

1.4.5 Recognize Meter in Time Signatures

Objectives and Assessment

- **Grade Level** - 4 - 12
- **Student Prerequisites** - Students should be able to accurately identify meter in heard music, and should understand the concept of written time signatures[48] in common notation[49].
- **Teacher Expertise** - The teacher must be knowledgeable about basic aspects of music reading and performance.
- **Time Requirements** - If you have plenty of music, this activity may take one (approximately 45-minute) class period. It may also be done as a short (5-15-minute) warm-up to other music activities or as a break from desk work, or you may do it with Listen for Meter (Section 1.4.2: Listen for Meter) or Sing with Meter (Section 1.4.3: Sing with Meter) to fill one class period.
- **Objectives** - The student will accurately identify the meter of a piece of music presented aurally, and will write a time signature that would be appropriate for the heard meter.
- **Extensions** - Advanced students can be given difficult examples: pieces with unusual meter (such as 5/4), complex or subtle rhythms, mixed meter, or borrowed meters.
- **Evaluation** - Assess student learning by grading written answers. For testing purposes, choose pieces with a clear and unchanging meter, and play or sing each selection for a reasonable length of time.

Procedure

1. Identify each piece by name, or assign each a number or letter. Have the students write down the name, number, or letter of each piece.

---

[48]"Time Signature" <http://cnx.org/content/m10956/latest/>
[49]"The Staff" <http://cnx.org/content/m10880/latest/>

2. Once they have identified the meter of a piece (in Listen for Meter (Section 1.4.2: Listen for Meter) or Sing with Meter (Section 1.4.3: Sing with Meter), or this may also be part of the written assignment), ask them to write down, next to its name, number, or letter, a possible time signature for it. Note that there will be several possible correct answers, although some may be more likely than others. Can they identify more than one possible time signature for the same meter?
3. For an added level of difficulty, identify a rhythm in the piece and ask them to write the rhythm correctly in the time signature they have chosen.
4. You may also want to ask: does the melody of each piece begin on "one", or are there pickup notes[50]?

1.5 Tempo[51]

The **tempo** of a piece of music is its speed. There are two ways to specify a tempo. Metronome markings are absolute and specific. Other tempo markings are verbal descriptions which are more relative and subjective. Both types of markings usually appear above the staff, at the beginning of the piece, and then at any spot where the tempo changes. Markings that ask the player to deviate slightly from the main tempo, such as ritardando (Gradual Tempo Changes, p. 14) may appear either above or below the staff.

1.5.1 Metronome Markings

Metronome markings are given in beats per minute. They can be estimated using a clock with a second hand, but the easiest way to find them is with a **metronome**, which is a tool that can give a beat-per-minute tempo as a clicking sound or a pulse of light. Figure 1.2 shows some examples of metronome markings.

---

[50]"Pickup Notes and Measures" <http://cnx.org/content/m12717/latest/>
[51]This content is available online at <http://cnx.org/content/m11648/1.6/>.

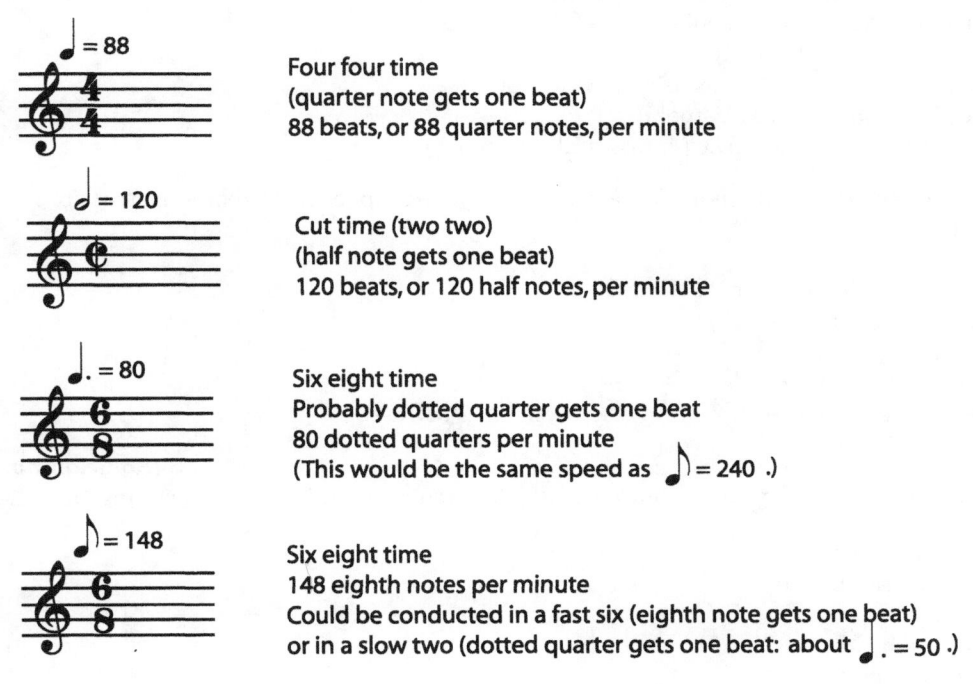

Figure 1.2

Metronomes often come with other tempo indications written on them, but this is misleading. For example, a metronome may have *allegro* marked at 120 beats per minute and *andante* marked at 80 beats per minute. *Allegro* should certainly be quite a bit faster than *andante*, but it may not be exactly 120 beats per minute.

1.5.2 Tempo Terms

A tempo marking that is a word or phrase gives you the composer's idea of **how fast the music should feel**. How fast a piece of music feels depends on several different things, including the texture and complexity of the music, how often the beat gets divided into faster notes, and how fast the beats themselves are (the metronome marking). Also, the same tempo marking can mean quite different things to different composers; if a metronome marking is not available, the performer should use a knowledge of the music's style and genre, and musical common sense, to decide on the proper tempo. When possible, listening to a professional play the piece can help with tempo decisions, but it is also reasonable for different performers to prefer slightly different tempos for the same piece.

Traditionally, tempo instructions are given in Italian.

Some Common Tempo Markings

- **Grave** - very slow and solemn (pronounced "GRAH-vay")
- **Largo** - slow and broad ("LAR-go")
- **Larghetto** - not quite as slow as largo ("lar-GET-oh")
- **Adagio** - slow ("uh-DAH-jee-oh")
- **Lento** - slow ("LEN-toe")
- **Andante** - literally "walking", a medium slow tempo ("on-DON-tay")

- **Moderato** - moderate, or medium ("MOD-er-AH-toe")
- **Allegretto** - Not as fast as allegro ("AL-luh-GRET-oh")
- **Allegro** - fast ("uh-LAY-grow")
- **Vivo, or Vivace** - lively and brisk ("VEE-voh")
- **Presto** - very fast ("PRESS-toe")
- **Prestissimo** - very, very fast ("press-TEE-see-moe")

These terms, along with a little more Italian, will help you decipher most tempo instructions.

More useful Italian

- **(un) poco** - a little ("oon POH-koe")
- **molto** - a lot ("MOLE-toe")
- **piu** - more ("pew")
- **meno** - less ("MAY-no")
- **mosso** - literally "moved"; motion or movement ("MOE-so")

Exercise 1.1 *(Solution on p. 25.)*

Check to see how comfortable you are with Italian tempo markings by translating the following.

1. un poco allegro
2. molto meno mosso
3. piu vivo
4. molto adagio
5. poco piu mosso

Of course, tempo instructions don't have to be given in Italian. Much folk, popular, and modern music, gives instructions in English or in the composer's language. Tempo indications such as "Not too fast", "With energy", "Calmly", or "March tempo" give a good idea of how fast the music should feel.

1.5.3 Gradual Tempo Changes

If the tempo of a piece of music suddenly changes into a completely different tempo, there will be a new tempo given, usually marked in the same way (metronome tempo, Italian term, etc.) as the original tempo. Gradual changes in the basic tempo are also common in music, though, and these have their own set of terms. These terms often appear below the staff, although writing them above the staff is also allowed. These terms can also appear with modifiers (More useful Italian, p. 14) like *molto* or *un poco*. You may notice that there are quite a few terms for slowing down. Again, the use of these terms will vary from one composer to the next; unless beginning and ending tempo markings are included, the performer must simply use good musical judgement to decide how much to slow down in a particular *ritardando* or *rallentando*.

Gradual Tempo Changes

- **accelerando** - (abbreviated *accel.*) accelerating; getting faster
- **ritardando** - (abbrev. *rit.*) slowing down
- **ritenuto** - (abbrev. *riten.*) slower
- **rallentando** - (abbrev. *rall.*) gradually slower
- **rubato** - don't be too strict with the rhythm; while keeping the basic tempo, allow the music to gently speed up and relax in ways that emphasize the phrasing
- **poco a poco** - little by little; gradually
- **Tempo I** - ("tempo one" or "tempo primo") back to the original tempo (this instruction usually appears above the staff)

1.6 A Tempo Activity[52]

An introduction to the concept of tempo, and lists of terms, can be found in Tempo (Section 1.5). To introduce the concept and some common tempo indications to younger students, try the following activity.

Goals and Standards

- **Goals** - The student will become familiar with the most common tempo terms and respond appropriately when asked to perform at a specific tempo indication, or to name a tempo indication for a performance just given or heard.
- **Grade Level** - The activity is designed for grades 3-8, but may be adapted for older or younger students as appropriate.
- **Student Prerequisites** - Whether singing, singing with gestures, dancing, or playing instruments, students should be able to perform the piece(s) adequately before doing this activity. Choose pieces and performance modes that are comfortable, so that the students can concentrate on tempo.
- **Teacher Expertise** - Teacher expertise in music is not necessary to present this activity. The teacher should be familiar and comfortable with the terms and concepts regarding tempo (Section 1.5), and should be comfortable leading the performance at various tempos.
- **Time Requirements** - If you wish to spend an entire class period on the activity, make certain you have enough pieces and tempos, and include the discussion of metronomes. A short demonstration of tempos will only take 15-20 minutes, or you can use the activity as a very short (just one piece, one or two tempos, each time) 5-minute warm-up to music class or active break from desk work.
- **Music Standards Addressed** - National Standards for Music Education[53] standards 1 (singing, alone and with others, a varied repertoire of music) or 2 (performing on instruments, alone and with others, a varied repertoire of music), and 6 (listening to, analyzing, and describing music).
- **Other Subjects Addressed** - The activity also addresses National Dance Standards[54] standard 1 (identifying and demonstrating movement elements and skills in performing dance).
- **Objectives** - The students will learn the meaning of the common tempo indications chosen by the teacher. As a group, the students will perform at least one piece (singing, singing with gestures, dancing, or playing instruments) at different tempos that are appropriate for the tempo markings they are learning. Given a piece and a tempo, the student will choose an appropriate tempo marking to describe it.
- **Evaluation** - Assess students on ability to maintain a steady beat at different tempos and on knowledge of tempo terms. To test knowledge following the activity, either ask individual students to indicate (by clapping a beat, for example), what speed they would choose given a certain tempo marking, or ask them to name an appropriate tempo while they listen to a recorded piece of music.
- **Follow-up** - Help commit this lesson to long-term memory, by continuing to ask, through the rest of the school year, "what tempo term would you use to describe the song we just sang?" and similar questions.

Materials and Preparation

- Decide which tempo indications (see Tempo (Section 1.5)) you would like the students to learn.
- Choose a simple song, song with gestures and dance steps, or dance, or a piece of instrumental music. (Or you may wish to choose more than one.) Choose pieces the students already know, or teach them the one(s) you have chosen before doing this activity.
- If you are going to discuss metronome markings, bring a metronome to class.
- If you are going to test the students following the activity using recordings, choose a variety of recordings.

Procedure

---

[52]This content is available online at <http://cnx.org/content/m14180/1.5/>.
[53]http://menc.org/resources/view/national-standards-for-music-education
[54]http://www.pecentral.org/lessonideas/dance/dancestandards.html

- Write your chosen terms and their meanings on the board, or give the students a handout with the terms, and go over them with the students.
- Have them sing, play, or dance the chosen piece(s) at different tempos (*allegro, largo, vivo*, etc.). Include variations in the tempo, such as *accelerando* if you like.
- If you are using more than one piece for this activity, try each piece at several different tempos. You may choose a "tempo marking", or have students take turns suggesting them. Have the students vote, or reach a consensus on, an appropriate actual tempo for each tempo indication suggested (with direction from you as necessary), and after trying several, have them vote on the best tempo marking for each piece.
- Most children love to play with metronomes. If there is one available, you may also want to discuss metronome markings. Try each chosen piece at several different metronome markings suggested by the students, and then ask them to choose a metronome marking for each piece. Discuss which tempo marking (*allegro, largo, vivo, andante*, etc.) they would assign that metronome marking for that piece. They may also enjoy trying to guess at which number the metronome was set.

Activity Extensions for Advanced Students

- Have the students learn a variety of the less common tempo terms.
- Help them explore what it means for a piece to feel fast or slow. Find recordings of (or have the students perform) different pieces that have the same tempo marking but noticeably different actual tempos. (Use a metronome to determine actual tempos.) Discuss the possible reasons for the differences. Are they cultural or historical? Are they affected by the style or genre of the music, the rhythms or the number of notes per beat?

1.7 Dynamics and Accents in Music[55]

1.7.1 Dynamics

Sounds, including music, can be barely audible, or loud enough to hurt your ears, or anywhere in between. When they want to talk about the loudness of a sound, scientists and engineers talk about amplitude[56]. Musicians talk about **dynamics**. The amplitude of a sound is a particular number, usually measured in decibels, but dynamics are relative; an orchestra playing *fortissimo* is going to be much louder than a single violin playing *fortissimo*. The exact interpretation of each dynamic marking in a piece of music depends on:

- comparison with other dynamics in that piece
- the typical dynamic range for that instrument or ensemble
- the abilities of the performer(s)
- the traditions of the musical genre being performed
- the acoustics of the performance space

Traditionally, dynamic markings are based on Italian words, although there is nothing wrong with simply writing things like "quietly" or "louder" in the music. *Forte* means loud and *piano* means soft. The instrument commonly called the "piano" by the way, was originally called a "pianoforte" because it could play dynamics, unlike earlier popular keyboard instruments like the harpsichord.

---
[55]This content is available online at <http://cnx.org/content/m11649/1.7/>.
[56]"Acoustics for Music Theory": Section Wave Amplitude and Loudness <http://cnx.org/content/m13246/latest/#s12>

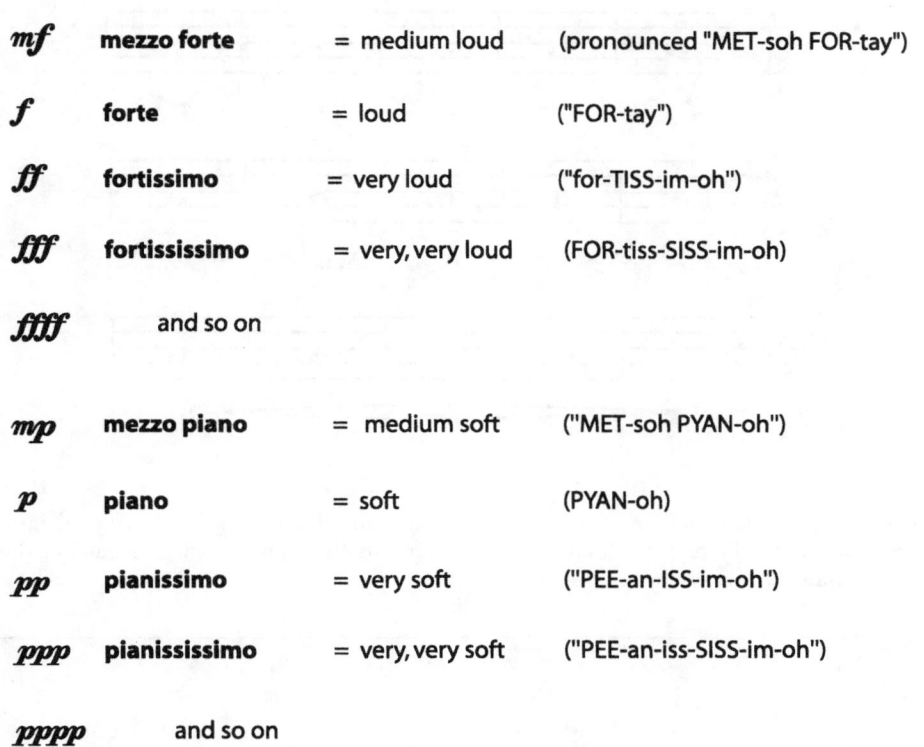

Figure 1.3

When a composer writes a *forte* into a part, followed by a *piano*, the intent is for the music to be quite loud, and then suddenly quite soft. If the composer wants the change from one dynamic level to another to be gradual, different markings are added. A *crescendo* (pronounced "cresh-EN-doe") means "gradually get louder"; a *decrescendo* or *diminuendo* means "gradually get softer".

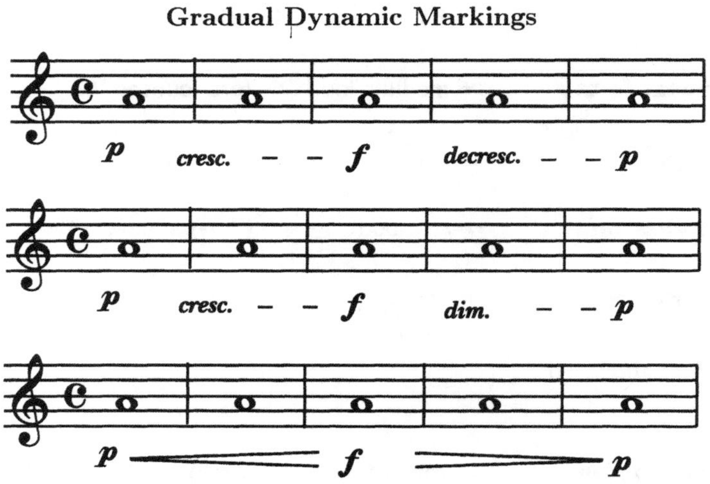

Gradual Dynamic Markings

Figure 1.4: Here are three different ways to write the same thing: start softly (piano), gradually get louder (crescendo) until the music is loud (forte), then gradually get softer (decrescendo or diminuendo) until it is soft (piano) again.

1.7.2 Accents

A composer may want a particular note to be louder than all the rest, or may want the very beginning of a note to be loudest. **Accents** are markings that are used to indicate these especially-strong-sounding notes. There are a few different types of written accents (see Figure 1.5 (Common Accents)), but, like dynamics, the proper way to perform a given accent also depends on the instrument playing it, as well as the style and period of the music. Some accents may even be played by making the note longer or shorter than the other notes, in addition to, or even instead of being, louder. (See articulation[57] for more about accents.)

Common Accents

Figure 1.5: The exact performance of each type of accent depends on the instrument and the style and period of the music, but the *sforzando* and *fortepiano*-type accents are usually louder and longer, and more likely to be used in a long note that starts loudly and then suddenly gets much softer. *Caret*-type accents are more likely to be used to mark shorter notes that should be stronger than unmarked notes.

---

[57]"Articulation" <http://cnx.org/content/m11884/latest/>

1.8 A Musical Dynamics Activity[58]

Practicing dynamics on a particular instrument requires control and technique, but simply learning about dynamics is an invitation to make noise, so this is a fun concept to introduce to young children. Practicing dynamics away from one's instrument can also be useful for young players who find it difficult to remember to play with dynamics and good tone quality because they are still mastering rhythms and fingerings.

Goals and Standards

- **Grade Level** - Intended for grades 3-8; adaptable for younger or older as appropriate.
- **Student Prerequisites** - Students should be able to sing, well and comfortably, the songs chosen.
- **Teacher Expertise** - Teacher expertise in music is not necessary to present this activity. The teacher should be familiar with the terms and concepts regarding dynamics (Section 1.7) and comfortable leading the singing.
- **Time Requirements** - If you want to give everyone a chance to "conduct", have a variety of several songs ready to sing, and plan to use an entire class period. Otherwise, the discussion and activity can be done in about twenty minutes. Once the concepts are introduced, you may use it as a short (5-minute) warm-up to other music activities or break from desk work.
- **Goals** - The student will learn standard terms for musical dynamics, explore using dynamics, and practice singing musically and with control at a variety of different dynamic levels.
- **Objectives** - The student will learn the terms used to indicate musical dynamics and will sing familiar songs with a group, at a variety of dynamic levels, responding first to verbal instructions from the teacher and then to hand signals from a "conductor". Following the activity, the student will be able to define common dynamics terms in simple English (e.g. *forte* is "loud") and respond to verbal or hand signals with appropriate dynamics.
- **Music Standards Addressed** - National Standards for Music Education[59] standards 1 (singing, alone and with others, a varied repertoire of music) and 6 (listening to, analyzing, and describing music).
- **Evaluation** - Assess students on achievement of many different dynamics while still singing with good tone, and on ability to follow conductor's dynamic directions. Following the activity, you may test the students, verbally or on paper, on the meaning of dynamics terms.
- **Follow-up** - Throughout the rest of the year, continue to ask for appropriate dynamics, using the correct terms, whenever the students sing or play an instrument.
- **Adaptations** - For students who have trouble singing, you may adapt this activity to have them recite, speak, or make noise on simple percussion instruments[60] at different dynamic levels.
- **Extensions** - For more advanced music students, have the students memorize a short piece on an instrument and practice responding quickly to instructions or signals to play at different dynamic levels. Teach the students notation for dynamics and ask them to play or sing, individually, a simple piece with no written dynamics, adding dynamics to make the performance more musical, interesting and dramatic. On the written part, have them add the (properly notated) dynamics that they are using.

Materials and Preparation

- Choose a song or songs that the students already know, or teach them one that is easy for them. Any song will do, although one with some dramatics that suggest dynamics may be more fun. Choose a song that is reasonably short, or else do the verses at different dynamic levels.
- Familiarize yourself with any dynamics (Section 1.7) terms that you are planning on introducing to the students. You may use this PDF file[61] as a handout if you would like to give the students a copy of the terms. (If you can't get the PDF file, you may use the figure below (Figure 1.6).)

---

[58]This content is available online at <http://cnx.org/content/m13463/1.5/>.
[59]http://menc.org/resources/view/national-standards-for-music-education
[60]"Percussion Fast and Cheap" <http://cnx.org/content/m11889/latest/>
[61]http://cnx.org/content/m13463/latest/pf.pdf

Procedure

1. Tell your students that music can be loud or soft or in between. Introduce any of the terms you wish your students to learn, or simply continue to talk about loud, soft, and medium.
2. Sing the song together softly (*mezzo piano*). Sing it again (or the next verse) even more softly (*piano*). Encourage them to continue to project voiced (not whispered) notes with clear, sustained pitch[62] as they get softer. Repeat until they are practically whispering; how many different levels of soft can they get while still sounding good?
3. Repeat the previous step with *mezzo forte*, *forte*, and so on. Encourage them to sing with sustained, controlled notes as they get louder. How many different levels of loudness can they get before they are simply shouting?
4. The next step will need a "conductor". You can conduct, but if there is time, let the students take turns conducting. Choose a conductor and demonstrate some typical conducting signals: hand held higher with palm up means louder, hand held lower with palm held down means softer, hand moving up or down means gradually louder or softer. **The conductor in this activity does not have to conduct the beats!**
5. Repeat the song again, or choose a different song if you're bored. This time, have the conductor vary the level of loudness during the verse. Try suddenly loud and suddenly soft as well as gradually getting louder and softer. For younger students, let them have fun with this and be silly. With older students, ask them to experiment with using the dynamics to make the song prettier or more exciting, dramatic, or interesting.

---

[62]"Pitch: Sharp, Flat, and Natural Notes" <http://cnx.org/content/m10943/latest/>

mf	**mezzo forte**	= medium loud	(pronounced "MET-soh FOR-tay")
f	**forte**	= loud	("FOR-tay")
ff	**fortissimo**	= very loud	("for-TISS-im-oh")
fff	**fortississimo**	= very, very loud	(FOR-tiss-SISS-im-oh)
ffff	and so on		
mp	**mezzo piano**	= medium soft	("MET-soh PYAN-oh")
p	**piano**	= soft	(PYAN-oh)
pp	**pianissimo**	= very soft	("PEE-an-ISS-im-oh")
ppp	**pianississimo**	= very, very soft	("PEE-an-iss-SISS-im-oh")
pppp	and so on		

Figure 1.6

1.9 A Musical Accent Activity[63]

See Dynamics and Accents in Music (p. 18) for introductory information on musical accents. The proper method for performing an accent varies greatly between different types of instruments and styles of music, and can present quite a challenge for the young instrumentalist. By temporarily separating reading from concerns on how to properly perform accents on a specific instrument, this activity simplifies the task of reading and performing "accents", allowing an intermediate success that can translate into confidence in performing accents correctly.

Goals and Evaluation

[63]This content is available online at <http://cnx.org/content/m13462/1.6/>.

- **Goals** - The goal of the activity is to introduce students to the concept of musical accents and to help beginning instrumentalists practice reading and performing accents.
- **Objectives** - The student will read notated rhythms - of gradually increasing complexity - that include accented notes, and perform them accurately as a simple percussion piece, either individually or with a group.
- **Grade Level** - This activity is designed for students in grades 4-8, but may be used by younger or older students who are at the appropriate level of musical awareness.
- **Student Prerequisites** - The students should be able to accurately and easily read and perform the rhythms in the exercises used.
- **Teacher Expertise** - The teacher should be able to read music well and must be able to act as the group "conductor" during this activity.
- **Time Requirements** - Unless you have many rhythm/accent examples prepared, this activity takes less than twenty minutes. Once the concepts are introduced, it can also be used as a very short (less than five minute) warm-up to other music activities or as a quick break from desk work.
- **Music Standards Addressed** - National Standards for Music Education[64] standard 5 (reading and notating music).
- **Adaptations** - To introduce the concept of accents to very young or non-reading students, simply alter the lesson plan to have the students echo short, simple rhythms with accents that are performed for them. This "listening and performing" activity may also be included along with the activity as described.
- **Extensions** - Following the activity, musically experienced students may be asked to write out short exercises similar to the ones they have already done. Share them by copying them or having the students write them so that the entire class can see them (on a board, for example). Let the class try the student-written exercises. Or let them trade papers with each other and perform each other's challenges as solos.
- **Evaluation** - Assess students on ability to read and perform rhythms and accents accurately and consistently, either with the group or individually in a "test" performance. If students can perform at the desired level of complexity, they are ready to practice performing accents in the proper manner on real instruments. If they cannot, have them continue to do this activity regularly over a period of weeks or months, starting with easier rhythms and gradually introducing more complexity, alternating with lessons on playing accents correctly.

Materials and Preparation

1. Prepare your board or a handout by reproducing the rhythms and accents below and/or making up your own, based on your students' age and musical training. You can copy this PDF file[65], or use the figure below (Figure 1.7: Accent Activity Suggested Rhythms) to make a handout. If you want an activity that will last longer, make up more lines at the correct difficulty level for your students.
2. Level I is for students who are younger and have little or no musical training. Level II is for students who have learned to read music. Level III is even more challenging.
3. Decide how the rhythms will be performed. Students can play on drums or other percussion instruments, if available, or play on a single pitch[66] on any instrument. You may also use body percussion or other simple percussion techniques (see Percussion Fast and Cheap[67]); for example clapping on regular notes and stomping, slapping thighs, or just clapping louder on accented notes; or slapping the table (or a thigh) with one hand for regular notes and both hands for accented notes.
4. Gather or make any instruments or equipment the students will need.

Procedure

---

[64] http://menc.org/resources/view/national-standards-for-music-education
[65] http://cnx.org/content/m13462/latest/accentactiv.pdf
[66] "Pitch: Sharp, Flat, and Natural Notes" <http://cnx.org/content/m10943/latest/>
[67] "Percussion Fast and Cheap" <http://cnx.org/content/m11889/latest/>

1. Explain that accented notes are louder than the notes around them. Show them an accent on the board or handout. Notes with an accent mark should be louder. Explain how you want regular and accented notes to be performed in this activity. (See number 3 of "Preparation".)
2. Before starting each rhythm, you must establish a steady beat, in order to get everyone to start at the same time and the same tempo (Section 1.5). Clap four times before the students begin, or count steadily and crisply, "One, two, three, go", or use any method of "counting off" that your students are already accustomed to.
3. Start with a slow beat. Do one rhythm at a time, all together as a group. For more of a challenge for older students, speed up the tempo, or ask them to perform rhythms alone, either after they have heard them, or sight-reading.

Accent Activity Suggested Rhythms

Level I

1.
2.
3.
4.

Level II

1.
2.
3.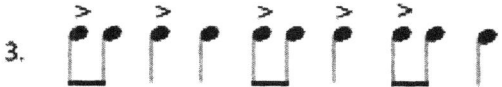
4.

Level III

1.
2.
3.
4.

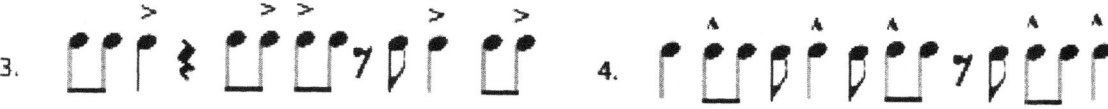

Figure 1.7

Solutions to Exercises in Chapter 1

Solution to Exercise 1.1 (p. 14)

1. a little fast
2. much less motion = much slower
3. more lively = faster
4. very slow
5. a little more motion = a little faster

Chapter 2

Pitch Elements

2.1 Timbre

2.1.1 Timbre: The Color of Music[1]

One of the basic elements of music is called **color**, or **timbre** (pronounced "TAM-ber"). Timbre describes all of the aspects of a musical sound that do not have anything to do with the sound's pitch[2], loudness (Section 1.7), or length[3]. In other words, if a flute[4] plays a note, and then an oboe[5] plays the same note, for the same length of time, at the same loudness, you can still easily distinguish between the two sounds, because a flute sounds different from an oboe. This difference is in the timbre of the sounds.

Timbre is caused by the fact that each note from a musical instrument is a complex wave containing more than one frequency. For instruments that produce notes with a clear and specific pitch[6], the frequencies involved are part of a harmonic series[7]. For other instruments (such as drums), the sound wave may have an even greater variety of frequencies. We hear each mixture of frequencies not as separate sounds, but as the color of the sound. Small differences in the balance of the frequencies - how many you can hear, their relationship to the fundamental pitch, and how loud they are compared to each other - create the many different musical colors.

The harmonics at the beginning of each note - the **attack** - are especially important for timbre, so it is actually easier to identify instruments that are playing short notes with strong articulations[8] than it is to identify instruments playing long, smooth notes.

The human ear and brain are capable of hearing and appreciating very small variations in timbre. A listener can hear not only the difference between an oboe and a flute, but also the difference between two different oboes. The general sound that one would expect of a type of instrument - a trombone[9] for example - is usually called its **timbre** or **color**. Variations in timbre between specific instruments - two different trombones, for example, or two different trombone players, or the same trombone player using different types of sound in different pieces - may be called differences in timbre or color, or may be called differences in **tone** or in **tone quality**. Tone quality may refer specifically to "quality", as when a young trombonist is encouraged to have a "fuller" or "more focussed" tone quality, or it can refer neutrally to differences in sound, as when an orchestral trombonist is asked to play with a "brassy" tone quality in one passage and a "mellow" tone quality in another.

---

[1]This content is available online at <http://cnx.org/content/m11059/2.8/>.
[2]"Pitch: Sharp, Flat, and Natural Notes" <http://cnx.org/content/m10943/latest/>
[3]"Duration: Note Lengths in Written Music" <http://cnx.org/content/m10945/latest/>
[4]"Flutes" <http://cnx.org/content/m12603/latest/>
[5]"The Oboe and its Relatives" <http://cnx.org/content/m12615/latest/>
[6]"Pitch: Sharp, Flat, and Natural Notes" <http://cnx.org/content/m10943/latest/>
[7]"Harmonic Series I: Timbre and Octaves" <http://cnx.org/content/m13682/latest/>
[8]"Articulation" <http://cnx.org/content/m11884/latest/>
[9]"Trombones" <http://cnx.org/content/m12602/latest/>

Many words are used to describe timbre. Some are somewhat interchangeable, and some may have slightly different meanings for different musicians, so no attempt will be made to provide definitions. Here are a few words commonly used to describe either timbre or tone quality.

- Reedy
- Brassy
- Clear
- Focussed or unfocussed
- Breathy (pronounced "BRETH-ee")
- Rounded
- Piercing
- Strident
- Harsh
- Warm
- Mellow
- Resonant
- Dark or Bright
- Heavy or Light
- Flat
- Having much, little, or no vibrato (a controlled wavering in the sound); or narrow or wide, or slow or fast, vibrato

For more information on what causes timbre, please see Harmonic Series I[10], Standing Waves and Musical Instruments[11], and Standing Waves and Wind Instruments[12].) For activities that introduce children to the concept of timbre, please see Timbre Activities (Section 2.1.2)

2.1.2 Timbre Activities[13]

Timbre, often called color, is one of the basic elements of music. Please see Timbre: The Color of Music (Section 2.1.1) for an introduction to the subject. You will find here suggestions for a Class Discussion and Demonstration of Color (Section 2.1.2.1: Class Discussion and Demonstration of Color), three simple Color Activities (Section 2.1.2.2: Color Activities), suggestions for Adapting or Extending the Activities (Section 2.1.2.3: Adaptations and Extensions), and Other Suggestions for Exploring Color (Section 2.1.2.4: Other Suggestions for Exploring Color).

Goals and Standards

- **Goals** - The student will learn to recognize timbre as a basic element of music, develop aural recognition of instruments, and learn appropriate terminology for discussing and evaluating this aspect of musical performances.
- **Grade Level** - PreK-12.
- **Student Prerequisites** - No prior student knowledge necessary.
- **Teacher Expertise** - Teacher expertise in music is not necessary to present this activity. The teacher should be familiar and comfortable with the terms and concepts regarding timbre. (See Timbre: The Color of Music (Section 2.1.1).)
- **Music Standards Addressed** - National Standards for Music Education[14] standards 6 (listening to, analyzing, and describing music), and 8 (understanding relationships between music, the other arts, and disciplines outside the arts). If instruments from other cultures are included in the examples, or if a discussion of the use of timbre to help identify the era or culture of a piece of music is included,

---

[10]"Harmonic Series I: Timbre and Octaves" <http://cnx.org/content/m13682/latest/>
[11]"Standing Waves and Musical Instruments" <http://cnx.org/content/m12413/latest/>
[12]"Standing Waves and Wind Instruments" <http://cnx.org/content/m12589/latest/>
[13]This content is available online at <http://cnx.org/content/m14259/1.3/>.
[14]http://menc.org/resources/view/national-standards-for-music-education

music standard 9 (understanding music in relation to history and culture) is also addressed. If students evaluate specific musical performances using references to timbre, music standard 7 (evaluating music and music performances) is also addressed.
- **Other Subjects Addressed** - The activity also addresses National Standards for Art Education in the Visual Arts[15] standard 6 (making connections between visual arts and other disciplines).
- **Follow-up** - Help commit this lesson to long-term memory, by continuing to ask, through the rest of the school year, questions about timbre and instrument recognition in any musical examples presented to the class.

2.1.2.1 Class Discussion and Demonstration of Color

Objectives and Assessment

- **Time Requirements** - Excluding the pre-test, this activity can be done in one (approximately 45-minute) class period; or you may spread the lesson, including pre- and post-tests, into four or five fifteen-minute increments over the course of several days.
- **Objectives** - When presented with a recording, the student will learn to recognize and name the instruments heard.
- **Evaluation** - If formal assessment is wanted, have a post-lesson aural test. Present the students with recordings or excerpts they have not yet heard, of the instruments you have been studying. For the test, the instrument to be identified should be either extremely prominent, or the only type of instrument being played. Either number the excerpts as you play them and have the students write down the instrument heard for each number, or call on specific students to name the instrument aloud.

Materials and Preparation

- You will need an audio player in the classroom.
- You may want to give the students a pretest to determine what instruments you will focus on. If most students are unable to recognize, by sound, common orchestral instruments[16], you will probably want to begin with these, and perhaps with some instruments that will be familiar from popular music. If your class is already good at recognizing more familiar instruments, concentrate on introducing some lesser-known orchestral instruments, or perhaps some well-known historical or Non-Western [17] instruments.
- You will need tapes or CDs with 3-8 examples of different instruments playing either alone, or as a very prominent solo, or in groups of like instruments (some suggestions: an unaccompanied violin or 'cello sonata, or a string quartet; classical or electric guitar; banjo; piano; harpsichord; percussion ensemble or drum solo; bagpipes; brass quintet; trumpet or oboe concerto; jazz saxophone solo; recorder ensemble).
- Prepare a tape with short excerpts (1-2 minutes) of each instrument, or be able to find your chosen excerpts quickly on the CDs. Unless you are very confident of the students' abilities to distinguish different instruments, try to pick very different sounds.
- If you like, prepare a simple worksheet they can use to match each excerpt with the name and/or picture of the instrument. If your group is small, a book with pictures of instruments that they can point to will work. Or write the names of the instruments on the board, show pictures from a book, or discuss the instruments enough that the children have a good idea what the instrument choices are. Have other excerpts as demonstrations if you think that might be needed.

Procedure

---
[15] http://cnx.org/content/m14259/latest/ http://artsedge.kennedy-center.org/teach/standards.cfm
[16] "Orchestral Instruments" <http://cnx.org/content/m11897/latest/>
[17] "What Kind of Music is That?" <http://cnx.org/content/m11421/latest/>

1. Begin with a class discussion. Ask the students if they prefer black-and-white or color pictures? Pictures with just one color or with many colors? Tell them that one of the things that makes music more interesting, exciting and pleasant is also sometimes called "color". Explain that the color of the sound is what makes one instrument sound different from another. You can introduce the word **timbre** (pronounced "TAM-ber") to your students if you like, but musicians also use the word "color", so it is fine to simply talk about the "color" of the sound.
2. Hand out your prepared worksheet, show pictures of instruments, or write down their names on the board and discuss them.
3. Play the excerpts. See if the students can identify the instruments by listening to their color.
4. If they can't, identify the instruments for them, then let them try again with different excerpts from the same pieces, or different pieces on the same instrument or group of instruments.

2.1.2.2 Color Activities

Objectives and Assessment

- **Time Requirements** - Excluding presentations, all three activities can be done in a single (approximately 45-minute) class period; or spread them out over the course of several days, by doing three separate sessions of 15-20 minutes. The extra time required to present artwork to the teacher or to the class will depend on the number of students and time allowed for each presentation.
- **Objectives** - The student will learn to recognize timbre (color) as a basic element of music, and will learn the proper terminology for discussing this element. The student will also use imagination and creativity to find links between music and the visual arts.
- **Evaluation** - Assess students on their presentations/explanations of their artwork.

Materials and Preparation

- You will need an audio player in the classroom.
- You will need CDs or tapes of a variety of instrumental music. For these activities, don't forget the possibility of music from other cultures (such as native American flute, South American panpipe groups, steel drums, Indian sitar, etc.) The very unfamiliarity of the sounds may encourage more speculation and creativity.
- Each student will need drawing paper and drawing implements (crayons, markers, colored pencils) in a variety of colors.
- If you have not already presented the class discussion of timbre (Section 2.1.2.1: Class Discussion and Demonstration of Color), introduce the term to the students before doing these activities.

Activities

1. Have the students listen to excerpts of individual instruments. Ask them to imagine that they can see the sounds; and ask them what color each sound would be if they could see it. Try to encourage naming specific hues. Does a trumpet sound like fire-engine red, day-glo orange, lemon yellow? Is a bassoon sea green or lilac? These are exercises for the imagination. There are no right answers; different sounds affect people differently, and all answers should be respected.
2. Have the students listen to excerpts of instrumental music. Encourage them to come up with adjectives that describe the color of the instruments. Some words that musicians often use to describe color/timbre are: bright, dark, full, thin, warm, rich, reedy, rounded, edgy, breathy (pronounced BRETH-ee), scratchy, heavy, light, transparent, and intense. If your students have trouble coming up with adjectives, suggest some of these, but encourage them to come up with their own, too. If students independently come up with a timbre word that musicians often use, point this out and congratulate them on doing so; but point out that the use of timbre words is fairly informal, and coming up with their own is fine, too, particularly if they are good descriptions of the sound.

3. Have the students listen to longer excerpts of instrumental music. While listening, they should make a drawing of anything that the music makes them think of. The drawing can be abstract - circles of yellow connected by red squiggles - or representational - a garden in the sun. The students should then get a chance to present their picture and explain why the music made them think of those colors, shapes, or objects. Encourage explanations that link specific colors, shapes or objects to specific timbres in the music.

2.1.2.3 Adaptations and Extensions

The class discussion and demonstration may be **adapted for students with visual impairment** by substituting the touch, smell, or taste sensations for color. (For example, does a specific timbre remind the student of a smooth or rough surface, of a sour or sweet flavor, or of a flowery or musky scent?) For students who cannot see color at all, you may also include a discussion of the sensations that the students "substitute" in their imaginations when they hear a color word. (For example, do they associate the word "red" with a particular sound, texture, or emotional feeling?) If possible, introduce the instruments by touch as well as by sound.

Challenge students who have reached a higher level of musical knowledge and discernment to be able to name many instruments "by ear", including rare, historical, or non-Western instruments. Ask them to try to identify an audio recording (by era or culture) based on the timbres (instruments) heard. Ask them to evaluate specific performances (recordings, or their own singing or playing, or the singing or playing of their classmates) in terms of timbre.

Challenge older or gifted students to make high-level artwork that reflects other aspects of the music (for example, emotional content, historical or cultural context, texture (Section 3.1), form (Section 3.5)), as well as timbre. You may want to provide high-quality art materials for this, and have the students prepare a display of the artwork with a paragraph, written by the student, explaining the musical inspiration for specific aspects of the artwork.

2.1.2.4 Other Suggestions for Exploring Color

- Watch "Fantasia" or "Fantasia 2000" together. Point out that many aspects of the music affect the images the artists chose: melody, harmony, rhythm, loudness, tempo (how fast the music is going). Timbre also strongly affects some of the choices. For example, in the Mickey Mouse/Sorcerer's Apprentice sequence (in both movies), the reedy sound of the woodwinds is associated with the enchanted broomstick, while the more liquid sound of the string section is associated with water, and the crashing sound of cymbals turns into thunder and crashing waves. What other examples can the students spot of a particular sound color being associated with an image or character?
- To acquaint the students with the colors of specific instruments, take field trips to concerts where the students will be able to see which instrument is making which sounds. For students that are old enough or musically experienced enough to begin to learn the colors of all of the instruments of the orchestra, Britten's *Young Person's Guide to the Orchestra* is a great place to start. Many orchestras will feature this piece at a "young person's concert", and some of these concerts include an "instrument petting zoo", a chance for the students to get up close to the instruments. For younger children, a performance or recording of "Peter and the Wolf", which features fewer instruments, may be more appropriate.
- Older students who can recognize the timbre of most instruments may enjoy playing "name that instrument" with a piece of music that features many different instruments in quick succession. Some good choices for this game are Copland's *Rodeo*, the beginning of Stravinsky's *Le Sacre du Printemps* ("The Rite of Spring"), Beethoven's *Symphony No. 6*, and Holst's *The Planets*.

2.2 Melody

2.2.1 Melody[18]

2.2.1.1 Introduction

Melody is one of the most basic elements of music. A note is a sound with a particular pitch[19] and duration[20]. String a series of notes together, one after the other, and you have a **melody**. But the melody of a piece of music isn't just any string of notes. It's the notes that catch your ear as you listen; the line that sounds most important is the melody. There are some common terms used in discussions of melody that you may find it useful to know. First of all, the **melodic line** of a piece of music is the string of notes that make up the melody. Extra notes, such as trills and slides, that are not part of the main melodic line but are added to the melody either by the composer or the performer to make the melody more complex and interesting are called **ornaments** or **embellishments**. Below are some more concepts that are associated with melody.

2.2.1.2 The Shape or Contour of a Melody

A melody that stays on the same pitch[21] gets boring pretty quickly. As the melody progresses, the pitches may go up or down slowly or quickly. One can picture a line that goes up steeply when the melody suddenly jumps to a much higher note, or that goes down slowly when the melody gently falls. Such a line gives the **contour** or **shape** of the melodic line. You can often get a good idea of the shape of this line by looking at the melody as it is written on the staff, but you can also hear it as you listen to the music.

Figure 2.1: Arch shapes (in which the melody rises and then falls) are easy to find in many melodies.

You can also describe the shape of a melody verbally. For example, you can speak of a "rising melody" or of an "arch-shaped" phrase (Section 2.2.1.4: Melodic Phrases). Please see The Shape of a Melody (Section 2.2.3) for children's activities covering melodic contour.

2.2.1.3 Melodic Motion

Another set of useful terms describe how quickly a melody goes up and down. A melody that rises and falls slowly, with only small pitch changes between one note and the next, is **conjunct**. One may also speak of such a melody in terms of **step-wise** or **scalar** motion, since most of the intervals[22] in the melody are half or whole steps[23] or are part of a scale[24].

A melody that rises and falls quickly, with large intervals[25] between one note and the next, is a **disjunct** melody. One may also speak of "leaps" in the melody. Many melodies are a mixture of conjunct and disjunct motion.

---

[18]This content is available online at <http://cnx.org/content/m11647/1.7/>.
[19]"Pitch: Sharp, Flat, and Natural Notes" <http://cnx.org/content/m10943/latest/>
[20]"Duration: Note Lengths in Written Music" <http://cnx.org/content/m10945/latest/>
[21]"Pitch: Sharp, Flat, and Natural Notes" <http://cnx.org/content/m10943/latest/>
[22]"Interval" <http://cnx.org/content/m10867/latest/>
[23]"Half Steps and Whole Steps" <http://cnx.org/content/m10866/latest/>
[24]"Major Keys and Scales" <http://cnx.org/content/m10851/latest/>
[25]"Interval" <http://cnx.org/content/m10867/latest/>

Figure 2.2: A melody may show conjuct motion, with small changes in pitch from one note to the next, or disjunct motion, with large leaps. Many melodies are an interesting, fairly balanced mixture of conjunct and disjunct motion.

2.2.1.4 Melodic Phrases

Melodies are often described as being made up of phrases. A musical **phrase** is actually a lot like a grammatical phrase. A phrase in a sentence (for example, "into the deep, dark forest" or "under that heavy book") is a group of words that make sense together and express a definite idea, but the phrase is not a complete sentence by itself. A melodic phrase is a group of notes that make sense together and express a definite melodic "idea", but it takes more than one phrase to make a complete melody.

How do you spot a phrase in a melody? Just as you often pause between the different sections in a sentence (for example, when you say, "wherever you go, there you are"), the melody usually pauses slightly at the end of each phrase. In vocal music, the musical phrases tend to follow the phrases and sentences of the text. For example, listen[26] to the phrases in the melody of "The Riddle Song" and see how they line up with the four sentences in the song.

---

[26] http://cnx.org/content/m11647/latest/phrases1.mid

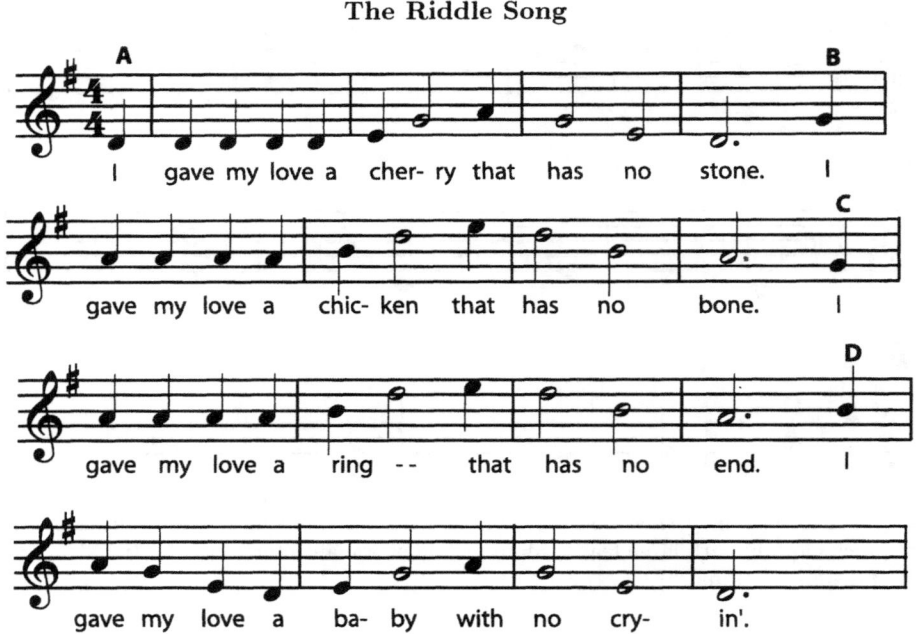

Figure 2.3: This melody has four phrases, one for each sentence of the text.

But even without text, the phrases in a melody can be very clear. Even without words, the notes are still grouped into melodic "ideas". Listen[27] to the first strain of Scott Joplin's[28] "The Easy Winners" to see if you can hear four phrases in the melody.

One way that a composer keeps a piece of music interesting is by varying how strongly the end of each phrase sounds like "the end". Usually, full-stop ends come only at the end of the main sections of the music. (See form (Section 3.5) and cadence[29] for more on this.) By varying aspects of the melody, the rhythm (Section 1.1), and the harmony (Section 2.3.1), the composer gives the ends of the other phrases stronger or weaker "ending" feelings. Often, phrases come in definite pairs, with the first phrase feeling very unfinished until it is completed by the second phrase, as if the second phrase were answering a question asked by the first phrase. When phrases come in pairs like this, the first phrase is called the **antecedent** phrase, and the second is called the **consequent** phrase. Listen to antecedent[30] and consequent[31] phrases in the tune "Auld Lang Syne".

---

[27] http://cnx.org/content/m11647/latest/phrases2.MID
[28] "Scott Joplin" <http://cnx.org/content/m10879/latest/>
[29] "Cadence in Music" <http://cnx.org/content/m12402/latest/>
[30] http://cnx.org/content/m11647/latest/antecedent.MID
[31] http://cnx.org/content/m11647/latest/consequent.MID

Antecedent and Consequent Phrases

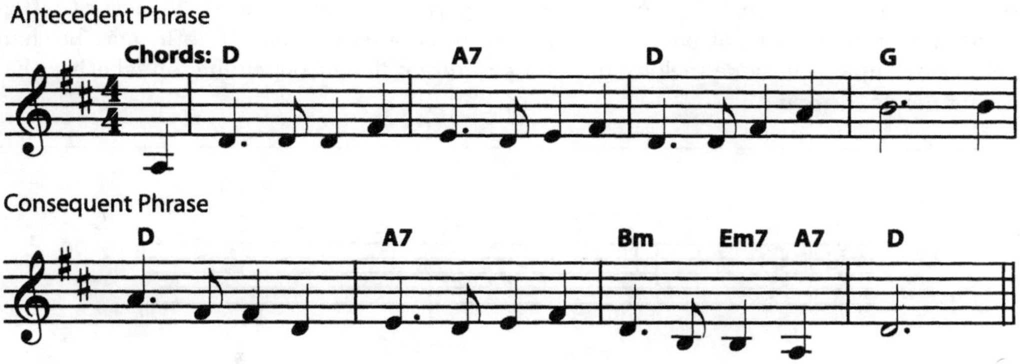

Figure 2.4: The rhythm of the first two phrases of "Auld Lang Syne" is the same, but both the melody and the harmony lead the first phrase to feel unfinished until it is answered by the second phrase. Note that both the melody and harmony of the second phrase end on the tonic[32], the "home" note and chord of the key.

Of course, melodies don't always divide into clear, separated phrases. Often the phrases in a melody will run into each other, cut each other short, or overlap. This is one of the things that keeps a melody interesting.

2.2.1.5 Motif

Another term that usually refers to a piece of melody (although it can also refer to a rhythm (Section 1.1) or a chord progression (Chords, p. 53)) is "motif". A **motif** is a short musical idea - shorter than a phrase - that occurs often in a piece of music. A short melodic idea may also be called a **motiv**, a **motive**, a **cell**, or a **figure**. These small pieces of melody will appear again and again in a piece of music, sometimes exactly the same and sometimes changed. When a motif returns, it can be slower or faster, or in a different key. It may return "upside down" (with the notes going up instead of down, for example), or with the pitches or rhythms altered.

Figure 2.5: The "fate motif"[33] from the first movement of Beethoven's Symphony No. 5. This is a good example of a short melodic idea (a **cell**, **motive**, or **figure**) that is used in many different ways throughout the movement.

---

[32]"Major Keys and Scales" <http://cnx.org/content/m10851/latest/#p1a>
[33]http://cnx.org/content/m11647/latest/motif1.mid

Most figures and motifs are shorter than phrases, but some of the *leitmotifs* of Wagner's operas are long enough to be considered phrases. A **leitmotif** (whether it is a very short cell or a long phrase) is associated with a particular character, place, thing, or idea in the opera and may be heard whenever that character is on stage or that idea is an important part of the plot. As with other motifs, leitmotifs may be changed when they return. For example, the same melody may sound quite different depending on whether the character is in love, being heroic, or dying.

Figure 2.6: A melodic phrase based on the Siegfried leitmotif[34], from Wagner's opera **The Valkyrie**.

2.2.1.6 Melodies in Counterpoint

Counterpoint (Section 3.3) has more than one melody at the same time. This tends to change the rules for using and developing melodies, so the terms used to talk about contrapuntal melodies are different, too. For example, the melodic idea that is most important in a fugue (Section 3.3.2: Some Useful Terms) is called its **subject**. Like a motif, a subject has often changed when it reappears, sounding higher or lower, for example, or faster or slower. For more on the subject (pun intended), please see Counterpoint (Section 3.3).

2.2.1.7 Themes

A longer section of melody that keeps reappearing in the music - for example, in a "theme and variations" - is often called a **theme**. Themes generally are at least one phrase long and often have several phrases. Many longer works of music, such as symphony movements, have more than one melodic theme.

---

[34]http://cnx.org/content/m11647/latest/motif2.mid

Theme from Beethoven's Symphony No. 9

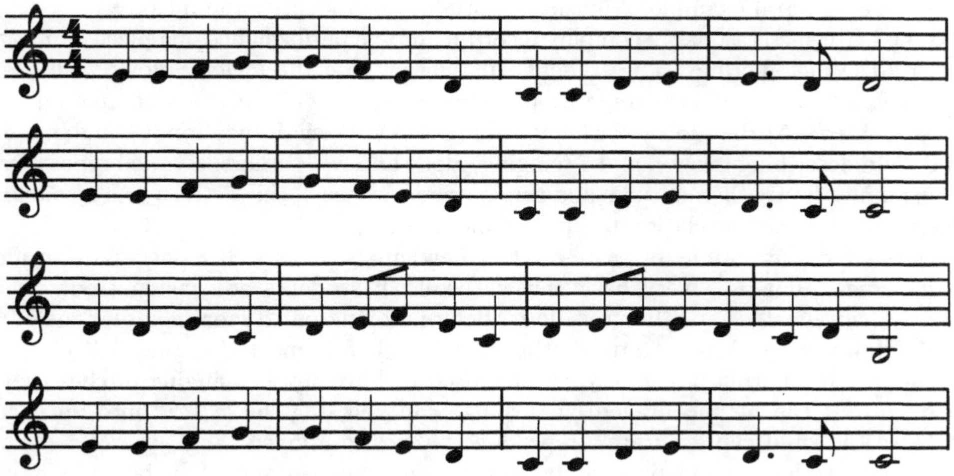

Figure 2.7: The tune[35] of this theme will be very familiar to most people, but you may want to listen to the entire last movement of the symphony to hear the different ways that Beethoven uses the melody again and again.

The musical scores for movies and television can also contain melodic **themes**, which can be developed as they might be in a symphony or may be used very much like operatic leitmotifs (p. 35). For example, in the music John Williams composed for the **Star Wars** movies, there are melodic themes that are associated with the main characters. These themes are often complete melodies with many phrases, but a single phrase can be taken from the melody and used as a motif. A single phrase of Ben Kenobi's Theme[36], for example, can remind you of all the good things he stands for, even if he is not on the movie screen at the time.

2.2.1.8 Suggestions for Presenting these Concepts to Children

Melody is a particularly easy concept to convey to children, since attention to a piece of music is naturally drawn to the melody. If you would like to introduce some of these concepts and terms to children, please see A Melody Activity (Section 2.2.2), The Shape of a Melody (Section 2.2.3), Melodic Phrases (Section 2.2.4), and Theme and Motif in Music (Section 2.2.5).

2.2 A Melody Activity[37]

Goals and Standards

- **Grade Level** - preK-5
- **Student Prerequisites** - none
- **Teacher Expertise** - Teacher expertise in music is not necessary to present this activity. The teacher should be able to set an example by humming or singing along with the examples.
- **Time Requirements** - 5-20 minutes, depending on the number of musical examples. You may want to do this activity as a short "listening warm-up" for a more involved melody activity, such as The Shape

---

[35] http://cnx.org/content/m11647/latest/Bninth.mid
[36] http://cnx.org/content/m11647/latest/motif3.mid
[37] This content is available online at <http://cnx.org/content/m11833/1.7/>.

of a Melody (Section 2.2.3), Melodic Phrases (Section 2.2.4), Theme and Motif in Music (Section 2.2.5), or A Musical Textures Activity (Section 3.2).

- **Goals** - Given an aural example of music, the student will identify the melody.
- **Objectives** - Given a reasonably complex recording or live performance of a piece of music, the student will identify the melodic line. The student will sing or hum the melody along with the recording or performance, and, after sufficient repetitions, hum or sing it without the accompaniment.
- **Music Standards Addressed** - National Standards for Music Education[38] standards 6 (listening to, analyzing, and describing music), and 1 (singing, alone and with others, a varied repertoire of music). If musical examples from other cultures and time periods are used, this activity can also address standard 9 (understanding music in relation to history and culture).
- **Evaluation** - Evaluate students on discussion participation, as well as accuracy in identifying and singing melodies. This is a very basic musical skill. If students are having trouble with it, repeat this activity periodically until they can do it, before moving on to more complex melody or harmony activities. (However, students can do rhythm activities before mastering this skill.)
- **Adaptations** - It's normal for very young children to have trouble singing pitches they hear; this is a learned skill. It can be encouraged by turning "can you sing this note?" into fun, age-appropriate games. Once the child can accurately reproduce pitches in a given range, search for melodies within that range. For students who have trouble hearing which line is the melody, begin by having them sing along with unaccompanied melodies or melodies with just rhythmic accompaniment. Add harmony parts later to let them hear how the melody interacts with the other parts.
- **Extensions** - Challenge musically advanced, gifted, or older students by presenting them with music from another time period or culture, or with complex instrumental music. Or you may ask them to find a part that is NOT the melody and sing along with that.

Materials and Preparation

- You can play the examples yourself, or have a performer play them for the class, or play recordings.
- Choose the music and the presentation method. Choose several pieces from different musical traditions, or with a variety of styles and melodies. Any music with a clear, singable melody that would appeal to children is good. For very young children or children with little musical experience, you may want to stick to music that is already familiar. For older or more musically experienced children, consider classical instrumental or Non-Western[39] music as well as folk, pop, and children's songs.
- Be ready to play the pieces, or have your tape or CD player ready, and have the tapes ready at the right spot or know the CD track numbers.

Procedure

1. Ask the students if they know what a melody is. They may know but be unable to give you a definition. Ask them to hum or sing an example of a melody. If they do not know what a melody is, explain that it is a musical line (a group of notes that comes one after the other) that normally gets most of your attention when you hear a piece of music, and that most people, when asked to sing or hum a piece of music, will give you the melody.
2. Starting with an easy melody, ask the students to listen while you play a short section of your chosen music.
3. Play the same section a second time, this time asking the students to hum or sing along with the melody.
4. Ask the students if any of them can sing or hum the melody to you without the music playing along. If they are shy, have them do it all together and/or with you. If they don't know it yet, have them listen to it again.

---

[38] http://menc.org/resources/view/national-standards-for-music-education
[39] "What Kind of Music is That?" <http://cnx.org/content/m11421/latest/>

5. You can begin to introduce some other musical concepts by asking them questions about the melody. Is it high or low? Is the highest note a lot higher than the lowest note or just a little higher than the lowest note (in other words, does it have a large or small range[40])? Does the melody jump quickly from high to low (**disjunct motion**), or does it move to notes that are not very much higher or lower (**conjunct motion**)? Are the notes long and connected to each other (**legato**) or short with space between them (**staccato**). Even young listeners may be able to answer some of these questions, which will encourage them to listen to the melody in an analytical way. Encourage them to mimic the style of the musical performance as well as the actual notes.
6. For older students, or students who are listening to instrumental examples, ask them which parts of the music are not melody. What instruments are playing the non-melody parts of the music? What instrument is playing the melody? Can they hum any of the non-melody parts, or clap the rhythms of a non-melody part? (This will be more difficult than identifying the melody.)
7. Repeat the activity with examples that gradually become more challenging.
8. Students for whom this is easy are ready to try identifying The Shape of a Melody (Section 2.2.3) finding Melodic Phrases (Section 2.2.4) or Theme and Motif in Music (Section 2.2.5), or identifying Musical Textures (Section 3.2).

2.2.3 The Shape of a Melody[41]

Melody is one of the basic elements of music, and one of the easiest to hear and understand. Melodies can soar, swoop, plunge, or hop around, and this activity encourages even very young listeners to listen carefully to a melody to hear what it's doing.

Goals and Assessment

- **Goals** - The student will learn to recognize basic information about a melody presented aurally, and discuss it using proper terminology.
- **Objectives** - The student will make visual representations of the lines of heard melodies. The student will explain verbally his own or others' visual representations of melodic line.
- **Grade Level** - preK-12 (adaptable)
- **Student Prerequisites** - Young students should be able to distinguish the melody when listening to music. Older and more musically experienced students will benefit most if the appropriate terms are introduced and/or some of the activity extensions are included.
- **Teacher Expertise** - Teacher expertise in music is not necessary to present this activity. The teacher should be familiar and comfortable with the terms and concepts regarding melody (Section 2.2.1).
- **Time Requirements** - One (approximately 45-minute) class period for the basic activity. One more class period for each of the extensions.
- **Music Standards Addressed** - National music standard[42] 6 (listening to, analyzing, and describing music) is directly addressed. You may also address standard 9 (understanding music in relation to history and culture) by including music from a variety of cultures or historical periods is used, and exploring the characteristics of typical melodies from other cultures or historical periods. If you are including a discussion of line in the visual arts or English language arts, (see Extensions (Extensions and Cross-Discipline Activities, p. 42), standard 8 is also addressed.
- **Other Subjects Addressed** See Extensions (Extensions and Cross-Discipline Activities, p. 42) for suggestions in English language arts, dance, and visual arts.
- **Evaluation** Assess students on accurate, useful portrayal of melodic concepts visually, as drawn lines, and on ability to use the correct terms in describing heard melodies or looking at visual renderings of them. If you wish, test the students by giving them short examples from music they have not yet heard, and ask them to describe it using the correct terms.

---

[40]"Range" <http://cnx.org/content/m12381/latest/>
[41]This content is available online at <http://cnx.org/content/m11832/1.4/>.
[42]http://menc.org/resources/view/national-standards-for-music-education

- **Follow-up** - Help this lesson get into long-term memories by continuing to ask the students, throughout the rest of the year, to describe the melodies that they are hearing, singing, or performing, using the correct terms.

Materials and Preparation

- See Melody (Section 2.2.1) for an introduction to the terms that you may introduce to your students with this activity. With very young or musically inexperienced students, you may want to only discuss the contour or shape of the melody. With older students, you may also want to introduce and discuss terms such as conjunct and disjunct motion (Section 2.2.1.3: Melodic Motion), melodic phrase (Section 2.2.1.4: Melodic Phrases), antecedent and consequent phrases (p. 34), motives or cells (Section 2.2.1.5: Motif), and/or counterpoint (Section 3.3) (particularly in terms of the contour-independence of true counterpoint lines). All of these concepts can be rendered as drawn lines.
- You will need some CDs or tapes of music with clear, obvious melodies, and something to play them on. Either vocal or instrumental music is fine. A selection of two or three pieces that have very different types of melody (for example, one with long, soaring melodies, one with short, clearly defined phrases, and one based on very short motifs) will get the best reaction from your students. Fairly short excerpts are probably all you will need.
- Each student will need paper to draw on and drawing implements. If you would like the students to also be free to express their interpretation of the color (Section 2.1.1) of the melodies, have them use crayons or markers.
- You will also need to be able to draw on a board or piece of paper, for demonstration purposes.
- Have your tapes ready at the correct spot for the melodies you have chosen, or know the track numbers of the CDs.
- For (older) students who are learning to read music, you may want to provide a copy of the written melody for at least one of your examples.
- For (older) students who are also studying the music of other cultures or time periods, include musical examples from the time period(s) or culture(s) being studied.
- If you are going to include a discussion of line in the visual arts, have some examples ready to show and discuss. You may use work done by the students in art class, original works by local artists, or reproductions of famous art work. A variety of styles, periods, and media, will be most helpful, particularly if the discussion will include stylistic differences in the use of line in the visual arts.
- If you are including a dance activity, you will need an open space for dancing. You may use the music that has been discussed and "drawn", or new music.
- If you are going to draw parallels with the language arts, have some poetry or other suitable selections ready for discussion.

Procedure

1. Ask your students to demonstrate high notes and low notes for you. Then ask for a volunteer to sing a few words of a song (or you sing a short phrase for them). Ask the class whether the notes in the example just sung are getting higher or lower. Explain that when the notes of a melody are getting higher, we say that the melody is going up. Draw a line for them, from left to right, that gets higher as it moves to the right. Draw another line for them that slopes down as it goes from left to right, for a melody that is going down. Your line can be straight, but curved lines often work better to connect contours together as the melody changes.
2. Have the students listen to a melody without drawing. Ask them if they can hear the melody going up or down. (You may want to ask them to "draw" an imaginary line in the air as they are listening.) Is it going up or down quickly (a steep line)? Does it go up and then down and then up again (maybe an arch with an extra curve up at the end)? Does it seem to stop and start again, or does it seem to be all connected together? Listen to the answers they give you, and demonstrate for them how you would draw that answer.

3. Now ask them to draw the "shape" or "contour" of some melodies for you. Let them use a fresh piece of paper for each new piece of music.
4. The interpretations may look very different from one student to the next. When drawing conclusions at the end of the session, try to emphasize the differences between the contours for different melodies rather than differences from one student to the next. Have the students describe the different melodies to you or to the class using their drawings as visual aids. Or allow other students to pick out which of a student's works represent which melody? Ask them how they can tell.
5. If you have provided a written example for students who can read music, hand out the written music after the students have already listened to the music and drawn its contour. Have them draw a contour shape over the written notes. Encourage them to draw a line that is smooth (not a connect-the-dots with the notes) but still follows the general rise and fall of the notes. Then have the students compare their freehand contour shapes with the ones that follow the written music. Can they find the similarities? If there are big differences, can they explain them?
6. If you are including musical examples from other time periods or cultures, discuss the conclusions the students would draw from these examples about what types of melodies are typical of each style of music.

The Riddle Song

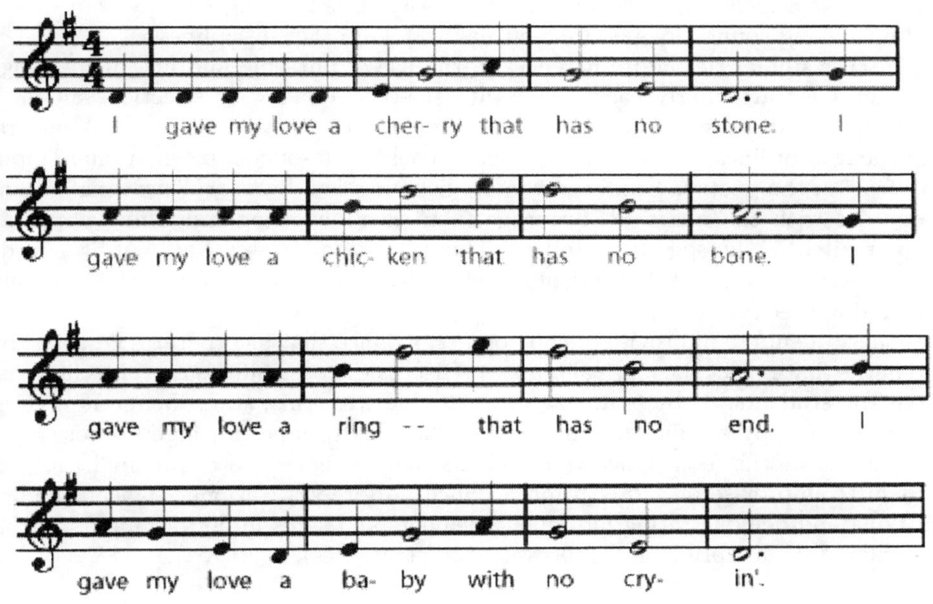

Figure 2.8: Here is an example of a simple melody. Listen[43] to the four phrases of "The Riddle Song".

---

[43]http://cnx.org/content/m11832/latest/phrases1.mid

Melodic Shape Example

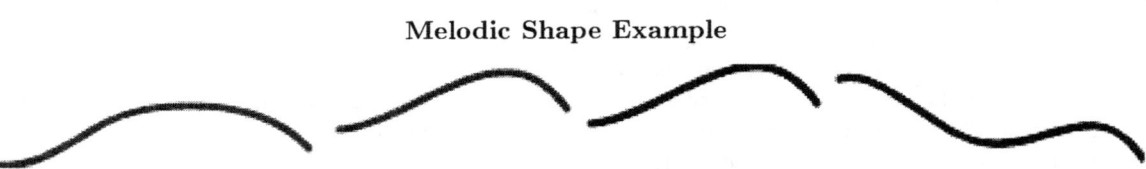

Figure 2.9: Here is one possible interpretation of the contours of the four phrases of The Riddle Song.

You can extend this activity, or use it to draw parallels between music and other disciplines.

Extensions and Cross-Discipline Activities

- **Visual Arts** - Discuss the similarities in the use of line and contour in music and in the visual arts. Show the students some examples from the visual arts. Discuss the use of line and contour in each of the examples. Do they rise and fall? Are they straight or curved? Short and choppy, or long and flowing? Is there anything in any of the artworks that acts as a motif? Do any of them have similarities to the any of the "musical phrase pictures" the students have produced? Might any similarities show cultural or historical preferences that are reflected in both music and the visual arts? This addresses National Standards for Art Education in the Visual Arts[44] standards 2 (using knowledge of structures and functions) and 6 (making connections between visual arts and other disciplines).
- **Language arts** - Discuss similarities and differences in the use of phrasing and line in the language arts and in music. This is particularly easy to do with poetry. Read your selections aloud, have students read them aloud, or have students memorize and deliver them "with feeling". What are the effects of the meter, length of lines, repetition of vowel or consonant sounds, or emotional emphasis, on the "sound" or "feel" of the poetry? Students who are listening could also try "drawing" the heard phrases just as they did with the music. (Encourage them to draw rising-and-falling phrases that follow the intensity or pitch of the speech patterns.) This activity addresses National Standards for the English Language Arts[45] standard 3 (Students apply a wide range of strategies to comprehend, interpret, evaluate, and appreciate texts).
- **Dance** - encourage the students to improvise or choreograph a dance that incorporates gestures, movements, shapes, and paths that reflect the musical phrases. Discuss the possibilities as a class first, asking for suggestions from the students. If the students have trouble with this, start them out with a few suggestions: for example, choppy motions for choppy melodies, high shapes for high sounds, repeated gestures reflecting musical motifs, etc. Once the students have a repertoire of possibilities, provide music and allow them to improvise or choreograph a dance. Addresses National Dance Standards[46] standards 1 (identifying and demonstrating movement elements and skills in performing dance) and 2 (understanding the choreographic principles, processes, and structures).

2.2.4 Melodic Phrases[47]

Here are lesson plans for two listening activities, Phrases in Songs (Section 2.2.4.1: Phrases in Songs) and Phrases in Instrumental Music (Section 2.2.4.2: Phrases in Instrumental Music), and one analysis/discussion activity, Parallels between Language and Musical Phrasing (Section 2.2.4.3: Parallels Between Language and Musical Phrasing), with some Suggested Music (Section 2.2.4.4: Suggested Music) for the activities.

Goals and Standards

---

[44]http://cnx.org/content/m11832/latest/ http://artsedge.kennedy-center.org/teach/standards.cfm
[45]http://cnx.org/content/m11832/latest/ http://www.ncte.org/about/over/standards/110846.htm
[46]http://www.pecentral.org/lessonideas/dance/dancestandards.html
[47]This content is available online at <http://cnx.org/content/m11879/1.4/>.

- **Grade Level** - 3-12
- **Student Prerequisites** - The student should be able to sing a song with others, and should be familiar with the language-arts definitions of sentence, phrase, and clause.
- **Teacher Expertise** - The teacher should be familiar and comfortable with the terms and concepts regarding melodic phrases (Section 2.2.1.4: Melodic Phrases), and should be able to easily identify musical phrases.
- **Goals** - The student will learn to identify melodic phrases (Section 2.2.1.4: Melodic Phrases) in vocal and instrumental music.
- **Music Standards Addressed** - Awareness of musical phrases helps the student sing and play with appropriate phrasing, (National Standards for Music Education[48] standards 1 and 2), and encourages the use of appropriate terminology in discussing music (standard 6).
- **Other Subjects Addressed** - The Parallels between Language and Musical Phrasing (Section 2.2.4.3: Parallels Between Language and Musical Phrasing) discussion encourages understanding of the relationship between language arts and music (National Standards for Arts Education music standard 8). It also addresses several of the National Standards for the English Language Arts[49], including reading literature from many genres (standard 2), drawing on understanding of textual features to appreciate texts (standard 3), and applying knowledge of language structure to discuss texts (standard 6).
- **Follow-up** - Help commit these lessons to long-term memory, by continuing to discuss phrasing when you introduce new pieces for the students to sing or play.

2.2.4.1 Phrases in Songs

Objectives and Assessment

- **Time Requirements** - With plenty of examples, this activity can take one (approximately 45-minute) class period. Or use fewer examples, and combine this activity with the next one in the same class period.
- **Objectives** - The student will listen to examples of vocal music and identify the phrases in the music.
- **Evaluation** - Assess students on their ability to accurately identify phrases in a "test" situation. Allow the students to listen to a short musical excerpt that the class has not yet discussed. Then play the excerpt again, calling on specific students to indicate by word or gesture when they hear the end of a phrase, or asking students to count the number of phrases in the example and write down their answers, or to write down the last word of each phrase. For the test, use music in which the phrasing is very clear, and not ambiguous at all, or allow for some reasonable disagreement if students can support their conclusions.

Materials and Preparation

- You will need an audio tape or CD player. Alternatively you can have the students supply the music by singing songs together that they all know or that they have been learning in class. (Simple songs like "The ABC Song", "Happy Birthday to You", or "The Itsy Bitsy Spider" work just fine for this activity.) You can plan on doing both, if you like.
- Gather some recordings of songs that your students will find appealing, or decide what songs you will have the students sing together. Folk music, church hymns, and traditional children's songs all usually have well-separated, easy-to-spot phrases. Some popular music and Classical music also works well, but some has more drawn-out, complex, or motive (Section 2.2.1.5: Motif)-based melodies that are difficult to separate into melodic phrases.
- For older students, if you would also like to introduce the concepts of antecedent and consequent (p. 34) phrases, make certain that some of your choices of music have clear antecedent/consequent-style phrasing.

---

[48] http://menc.org/resources/view/national-standards-for-music-education
[49] http://cnx.org/content/m11879/latest/ http://www.ncte.org/about/over/standards/110846.htm

- Have tapes ready to play at the right spot, or know the CD track numbers that you will be using. Or, if it would be helpful, have copies of the words to the songs the students will sing.

Procedure

1. Remind your students that language can be broken down into separate words, phrases, sentences, and paragraphs. (Remind them of what they have learned about these concepts in language arts.) Tell them that music is like a language: people compose music to say something to other people or make them feel a certain way. In the language of music, notes are like the letters of an alphabet, and they are grouped together into musical ideas that make sense to our ears, just like letters are grouped together into words, phrases, and sentences. (If you like, you may explain here that very short musical "words" that appear often in a piece of music can be called motives (Section 2.2.1.5: Motif), *motifs*, or **cells**, whichever term you prefer.) Groups of words that form a whole idea that makes sense may be a simple, complete sentence, or may be a major clause or phrase in a more complex sentence; groups of notes that make a whole musical idea that makes sense are called phrases. Just as you pause at the period at the end of the sentence (or at the comma at the end of a long phrase or clause), a melody also often pauses slightly when it comes to the end of a phrase. The phrases of the music are also grouped together into more complete ideas (particularly antecedent and consequent (p. 34) phrases, which may seem like two clauses in a long sentence, or like a question and answer), and/or into longer sections (a verse can be a section, for example) that are like paragraphs or even chapters. (See Form in Music (Section 3.5) if you would like your class also to study the larger divisions that are present in music.) Tell them that in songs, musical phrases often (but not always) line up with the sentences or phrases in the text. Share the two examples in Melody (Figure 2.3: The Riddle Song) if you like.
2. Have the students sing or listen to a song. You only need to study the first verse and refrain: even though the text changes, the musical phrases will be the same for each verse.
3. Play or sing the song again, asking the students this time to identify the first, second, third, etc. phrases, perhaps by singing them separately, raising their hands with the correct number of fingers at the start of a phrase, or just saying "two" at the beginning of the second phrase. You may have to sing or play the song several times to give them a chance to decide.
4. This should be a group activity, with reasonable disagreements allowed. Unless the phrases are extremely clear, some people will hear shorter sections of the melody as being distinct phrases, while others will naturally group the shorter sections into longer phrases.
5. Some questions to encourage further exploration: Are the phrases about the same length (the same number of beats), or are some much longer or shorter? Is a melodic phrase ever repeated exactly? Repeated with some changes? Do some phrases feel more final than others, as if they have a stronger ending? Where are the stronger endings located, and is there a pattern to them? Do some feel like they are a question waiting for the next phrase to answer them?

2.2.4.2 Phrases in Instrumental Music

Objectives and Assessment

- **Time Requirements** - Combined with Phrases in Songs (Section 2.2.4.1: Phrases in Songs), one (approximately 45-minute) class period.
- **Objectives** - The student will listen to examples of instrumental music and identify the phrases in the music.
- **Evaluation** - Assess students on their ability to accurately identify phrases in a "test" situation. Allow the students to listen to a short musical excerpt that the class has not yet discussed. Then play the excerpt again, calling on specific students to indicate by word or gesture when they hear the end of a phrase, or asking students to count the number of phrases in the example and write down their answers. For the test, use music in which the phrasing is very clear, and not ambiguous at all, or allow for some reasonable disagreement if students can support their conclusions.

Materials and Preparation

- If your students do "Phrases in Songs" successfully, let them try this activity.
- You will need a tape or CD player and some recordings.
- Try to choose instrumental music that also has singable melodies with clear, separated phrases. Bach and other Baroque composers are usually not a good choice, nor is most modern classical music or music based on shorter motifs, or music that is too complex.

Procedure

1. The procedure is essentially the same as for the previous activity. Let the students hum phrases to you if they can, or simply signal when they hear a new one.

2.2.4.3 Parallels Between Language and Musical Phrasing

Objectives and Assessment

- **Time Requirements** - one (approximately 45-minute) class period.
- **Objectives** - The student will study the text of a song, identifying (grammatical) sentences, phrases and clauses. The student will listen to the song, identifying musical phrases. The student will compare grammatical and musical phrasing, and draw appropriate conclusions.
- **Evaluation** - Analyze one text together, as a class. Then have the students do a second analysis individually, as a worksheet to be completed during the class period and turned in.

Materials and Preparation

- To do this activity, students must already be comfortable identifying musical phrases, and also identifying sentences, phrases, and clauses in texts.
- Choose a song or two to analyze for grammatical and musical phrasing. Art songs, madrigals, songs from musicals, and some rap, pop, and rock lyrics are all good sources for this, as well as folk songs, hymns, and children's songs.
- Obtain copies of the song text(s) for the students to look at. You may make handouts, for students to complete as a worksheet, or look at a projected copy of the text together and discuss as a class.

Procedure

1. Begin by analyzing the texts as the students have been doing in language arts. This may include identifying complete sentences, phrases, dependent and independent clauses, etc. If appropriate, you may also want to study the song lyrics as poetry texts, identifying metaphors, etc.
2. Have the students mark sentences, clauses, etc., on their handouts in whatever way is standard in their language arts class, or call on students to identify them aloud, while you mark the projected copy of the text.
3. Have the students listen to the song several times. Ask them to mark the musical phrases in a different way (or in a different color) than the grammatical phrases (or to signal where you should mark on the projected sheet). Play the song as many times as necessary to allow the students to decide where the musical phrases end.
4. Have the students compare the grammatical and musical phrasing as marked. Do they line up completely? If there are any places where they don't line up, what seems to be the reason for the disconnect? Is it related to the emotional content of the song? To certain aspects of the music or the text? Does the musical phrasing emphasize any aspect of the text (metaphors, questions, arrangement of clauses into sentences, etc.)?

5. If you are going to ask the students to analyze a second song individually, leave plenty of time for this, even if it means not finishing the analysis of your example. Do enough of the first example, as a group, to give them a clear idea of the procedure. Then give them 20 to 30 minutes (depending on the length of the song) to do their analysis of the second example, using the same marking style, and answering any questions you want included. Play the second song several times while they are analyzing and writing about it.

2.2.4.4 Suggested Music

Music that has clear phrases is very common, but there is some music in which phrases are harder to identify. In general, steer clear of Baroque counterpoint (Bach, for example), modern Classical music, the more complex styles of jazz, and late Romantic composers such as Mahler and Wagner. Folk songs, pop musics (including rock and country), children's songs, hymns, marches, dances, ragtime, opera arias, and symphonic music that has a clear melody are all good places to look. In case you're still not sure where to start, here are some suggestions that should be easy to find.

Some easy-to-find Instrumental Music with Clear Phrases

- Scott Joplin's "The Entertainer", or other ragtime tunes
- The Largo movement of Dvorak's *Symphony No. 9*
- The "March of the Toreadors" from Bizet's *Carmen*
- The "Waltz of the Flowers", "Chocolate (Spanish Dance)", "Tea (Chinese Dance)", or "Trepak (Russian Dance)" from Tchaikovsky's *The Nutcracker*
- Almost any popular march
- Most dixieland or swing-era jazz tunes

Vocal Music with Clear Phrases

- This is so easy to find there is no point in my listing particular pieces for you to look for. Most folk and popular vocal music has clear, separate, easy-to-hear phrases, as do most songs from musicals.

2.2.5 Theme and Motif in Music[50]

There are lesson plans here for four activities that promote aural recognition of, and understanding of the uses of, themes and motifs in music. Motifs (Section 2.2.5.1: Motifs) and Melodic Themes and Movies (Section 2.2.5.2: Melodic Themes and Movies) are appropriate for students of any age who can accurately recognize (by ear) a specific, short melody. (Students who are not quite ready for these activities may benefit from A Melody Activity (Section 2.2.2) and The Shape of a Melody (Section 2.2.3).) Opera Motifs (Section 2.2.5.3: Opera Motifs) will work best with older, more musically experienced students who have a longer attention span for serious music. Composing and Improvising Using Motifs (Section 2.2.5.4: Composing and Improvising using Motifs) is appropriate for students who are capable of playing an instrument and writing common notation fairly accurately.

Goals and Standards

- **Goals** - The student will learn to recognize when a repeated motif is being used in a piece of music (presented aurally), and will become familiar with some of the specific uses of musical motifs.
- **Music Standards Addressed** - These activities encourage the use of appropriate terminology in analyzing and describing music (National Standards for Music Education[51], music standard 6). If music from a variety of cultures or historical periods is used, and the discussion includes an exploration of the use of motifs in the music of different cultures or historical periods, music standard 9 is also addressed. The students may also be given a chance to compose (music standard 4) or improvise (music standard 3) using motifs.

---

[50]This content is available online at <http://cnx.org/content/m11880/1.4/>.
[51]http://menc.org/resources/view/national-standards-for-music-education

- **Other Subjects Addressed** - The Melodic Themes and Movies (Section 2.2.5.2: Melodic Themes and Movies) and Opera Motifs (Section 2.2.5.3: Opera Motifs) activities can easily be adapted to also address **English Language Arts** or a **foreign language** (if the opera is sung in another language), by including discussion of language use, plot, character, and the interaction of these elements with the music, and by including formal essays.
- **Follow-up** - Help this lesson get into long-term memories by continuing to ask the students, throughout the rest of the year, to identify motifs in music they are hearing or learning.

2.2.5.1 Motifs

Objectives and Assessment

- **Grade Level** - K-12 (adapt by using age-and-experience-appropriate musical examples)
- **Student Prerequisites** - Students must be capable of remembering and aurally recognizing a specific melody, even when some aspects of it have changed.
- **Teacher Expertise** - Teacher training in music is not necessary to present this activity. The teacher should be familiar and comfortable with the terms and concepts regarding motif (Section 2.2.1.5: Motif), and should be able to hear and point out the motifs in the music presented.
- **Time Requirements** - For one (approximately 45-minute) class period, have ready about 20 minutes of musical examples.
- **Objectives** - The student will recognize when and how a motif is used, when presented with an aural example.
- **Evaluation** - Assess student learning by evaluating class participation.

Materials and Preparation

- You will need an audiotape or CD player and a recording of a piece of music that is strongly based on a short, easily-heard motif. Some suggestions follow, or you can use your own favorites.
- If you have the class time, you may want to do two recordings, starting with a piece with more obvious motifs and ending with a piece in which the use of motifs is a little more subtle. Or if the class needs persuading that classical music is approachable, you may want to start with a non-classical piece and move on to a classical piece.
- Definitions and explanations of the concepts to be presented in this activity can be found at Melody (Section 2.2.1.5: Motif).

Some Easy-to-find Music Based on Motives

- The first movement of Beethoven's Symphony No. 5 has the most famous motive in Western classical[52] music.
- In "The Ride of the Valkyrie", from Wagner's opera *Die Walkuere* (*The Valkyrie*), there are two closely-related motives to listen for; the melody is built on one, and the accompaniment is built on the other. Most of Wagner's opera music is based on motifs, but there can be so many different motifs being used in one section of the music that they can be difficult to spot unless you are familiar with the opera. If you can't find "The Ride of the Valkyrie", try listening to the overture to *The Flying Dutchman* (*Die Fliegende Hollander*).
- All of the movements of Holst's *The Planets* are highly motivic, but each movement develops several different motives, and some are easier to spot than others. The rhythmic motive in "Mars" is by far the most obvious, but the four-note motive that opens "Uranus" is also very easy to hear. If you use this piece, you may want the further challenge of seeing how many different motives you can hear in a movement, as well as how each of them change. Are the melodic lines based on motives?

---

[52]"What Kind of Music is That?" <http://cnx.org/content/m11421/latest/>

- The five-note "alien message" motif in John Williams' score for "Close Encounters of the Third Kind" may already be familiar to some students. Many other movie and television scores also include short motifs (see below (Section 2.2.5.2: Melodic Themes and Movies)).
- Not all motivic music is classical in style; from early ragtime tunes like Joplin's "Maple Leaf Rag", through big band tunes like "String of Pearls" and "In the Mood", to the cool jazz of Miles Davis' *Kind of Blue*, to the latest improvised solo, jazz is full of motifs.
- Listen for the two-note "look down" motive from the work song at the beginning of *Les Miserables* to return throughout the musical. There are other motives in this musical, too, and in many other musicals (*Phantom of the Opera*, for example).
- Many other classical works are also full of motivic development, particularly works written in the late nineteenth or early twentieth century. Try listening to both the "Waltz of the Snowflakes" and "Coffee (Arabian Dance)" from Tchaikovsky's *The Nutcracker*, or to Strauss' tone poems ("Till Eulenspiegels Lustige Streiche", for example) or to the orchestral works of Stravinsky (for example, the first movement of the "Symphony in E Flat") or Dvorak (for example, the first and second movements of his "Symphony No. 9: From the New World"). If a piece has many motifs, you may not be able to keep track of all of them until you have heard the piece several times and are more familiar with it. Start by picking out one motif that you can hear and listening for it, or by simply counting motifs.

Procedure

- Introduce the concept of motifs to your students.
- Play a short excerpt (with plenty of examples of the motif) from your recording. Ask the students to hum or sing ("da da da DAH") the basic motif for you. Ask them if they heard any variations on the motif (perhaps slower or faster, with a change in the rhythm or in the pitches, or with an extra note or two, or maybe played "upside down" with the melody going up instead of down).
- Play a short excerpt for the students again (the same one, or a different excerpt from the same piece). Can they sing or describe any of the variations of the basic motif that they hear? Can they raise hands when they hear a variation?
- Play the entire recording (or a long section) asking the students to raise their hands each time they hear the motif, or to try to count how many times they hear it or a variation. Was only the one motif used throughout the piece, or did they hear any other motifs being used? If the students can identify more than one motif, divide the class into groups, one for each motif, and have each group raise their hands when they hear their particular motif.
- If you like, you can ask the students if they ever hear anything like a motif in the music that they usually listen to. Can they sing or hum the motifs for you, and tell you what style of music they are found in and how they are used? If you like, let them bring examples for the class to listen to. (If necessary, check them for suitability before playing them for the class.)

2.2.5.2 Melodic Themes and Movies

Objectives and Assessment

- **Grade Level** - K-12
- **Student Prerequisites** - Students must be able to aurally recognize specific melodies in spite of minor alterations or changes in texture (Section 3.1) or timbre (Section 2.1.1).
- **Teacher Expertise** - Teacher expertise in music is not necessary to present this activity. The teacher should be familiar and comfortable with the terms and concepts regarding motif (Section 2.2.1.5: Motif).
- **Time Requirements** - If you are very organized and also only show short excerpts, this activity can be done in one (approximately 45-minute) class period. You will find it easier to present the entire discussion, with plenty of time for watching/listening (and essay assignment) in a 2-hour time frame (or two separate class periods).

- **Objectives** - The student will practice actively listening for and recognizing specific motifs in a familiar musical setting.
- **Evaluation** - Grade students on active participation in the discussions, and on essays if assigned.

Materials and Preparation

- See Melody (Section 2.2.1.6: Melodies in Counterpoint) for a discussion of the terms and concepts that you may want to present to the students during this activity.
- Locate a videotape or DVD of a movie (that is appropriate for your students) with thematic music. "Star Wars Episode IV: A New Hope" is one of the best examples around, but other movie scores by John Williams (the "Indiana Jones" movies, for example) also tend to be very thematic, and so do many other adventure, fantasy, and science fiction films. (Serious dramas and comedies are less likely to use music in this way.) For younger children, one of the sections of "Fantasia" or "Fantasia 2000" may be used, although this is not ideal, since the pictures have been made to fit the music and not the other way around. Animated musicals that reuse melodic themes from some of the songs as background music during dramatic moments can also work. It's a good idea to choose a movie that many of your students are already familiar with; it can be difficult to be consciously aware of the music if you are very engrossed in the story.
- If you are only going to play part of the movie, decide ahead of time which part. Look for spots with lots of characters, lots of action, and plenty of background music. In this case, be ready to start the movie at your chosen spot.
- You will need the appropriate equipment for presenting the movie in class.

Procedure

1. If you have not already been discussing melody, motifs, and melodic themes in class, begin by reviewing some of these terms for them. (Use the discussion in Melody (Section 2.2.1.5: Motif) if you wish). If you are trying to encourage an appreciation of classical music, or if your class is preparing to attend an opera, point out that using "motifs" or different "theme" music for heroes, villains, rings, swords, love, or battles, was an old tradition in opera long before it was borrowed by movies and television.
2. Now discuss the movie. How many of the students have seen it? Who are the main characters? Are there "good guys" and "bad guys"? What's the main point of the plot; i.e. what are the main characters trying to do? Are there objects or ideas that are so important that they might get their own musical theme?
3. Once they have refreshed their memories about the movie, play some of the music for them without a picture and preferably without dialogue. The main title music or end title music is often a good place to hear the different themes. Or you can cover the TV screen or turn it away from the students and let them listen to the section of the movie that you are about to show.
4. As they listen, ask them if they recognize any of the melodic themes as belonging to certain characters. Is a certain melody "good guy music" or "bad guy music"? Is there a romantic theme or a heroic or danger theme? If they're not certain of specific associations, can they tell just from listening to it whether it's for "good guys" or "bad guys", "love" or "battle"? What are the musical difference between the different types of themes? (They can use simple descriptives for this, but encourage them to use any of the correct terminology they do know for various aspects of melody (Section 2.2.1), harmony (Section 2.3.1), texture (Section 3.1), timbre (Section 2.1.1), and rhythm (Section 1.1). (If it would be helpful, remind them of the terms they know by displaying them where all the students can see and refer to them.)
5. Remind them to try to be aware of the music while they are watching the movie. Ask them to notice how many different themes they can hear and how often they appear and who or what they belong with. Do you only hear them when a character is on the screen, or do you sometimes hear them as a warning that something is about to happen or even that someone is thinking about something?
6. Show the movie or part of it. When the music is particularly prominent during the movie, point out the melody and ask who or what they think that theme represents. Is it the same as always or has it

changed, perhaps to sound sadder, or sillier, or more exciting. If it changes, what is happening in the story to make the music change? If the students are too engrossed in the story, play one section of it repeatedly, to give them more of a chance to view it analytically.

7. After the movie, repeat the discussion in steps 3 and 4, to see if the students can now identify more of the themes.
8. Older students may be asked to write a short essay either summarizing the class discussion, or writing an analysis of the use of a particular motif in the movie (who or what it signifies, how and when it is heard, how it changes, etc.). If you want each student to write an individual analysis, explain the assignment and make sure the students can recognize the motifs they are listening for, then allow them to take notes as they watch the movie or section of the movie a final time. With older students, this can also become a take-home individual or group assignment, with the students watching a different movie than the one discussed in class. (If you are concerned about their choice of subject, have them pick a movie from a suggested list.)

2.2.5.3 Opera Motifs

Objectives and Assessment

- **Grade Level** - 8-12 (or younger with age-appropriate opera and adequate preparation)
- **Student Prerequisites** - Students should be capable of remembering and aurally recognizing specific melodies, regardless of small alterations in melody (Section 2.2.1), rhythm (Section 1.1), texture (Section 3.1), or timbre (Section 2.1.1). This activity will work best with students who have a mature attention span and some familiarity with classical music[53].
- **Teacher Expertise** - The teacher should be familiar and comfortable with the terms and concepts regarding motif (Section 2.2.1.5: Motif), and should be familiar with the opera to be presented, but training in music education is not necessary.
- **Time Requirements** - Allow at least 30 minutes each for pre-performance and post-performance discussions. Performance time will depend on specific opera and venue.
- **Objectives** - The student will practice actively listening for and recognizing specific motifs in opera music, and will understand the musical and dramatic uses of opera motifs.
- **Evaluation** - Grade students on active participation in the class discussion, and on essays if assigned.

Materials and Preparation

- You may want to prepare the class for this activity by doing the Motif and/or Melodic Themes and Movies (Section 2.2.5.1: Motifs) activities first. A lecture on the terms and concepts regarding motif (Section 2.2.1.5: Motif) is the minimum necessary class preparation for this activity.
- Arrange for the class to see a live opera performance performed locally, or to watch in class a taped opera performance. Whether live or taped, subtitles are important if the performance is in a foreign language.
- See Melody (Section 2.2.1.5: Motif) for a discussion of the concepts and terms that you may want to introduce to the students before seeing the opera.
- If this is a production by a local company, the easiest way to do this may be to contact the opera company and ask if they have anyone who does or is willing to do outreach or education programs. Ask for a presentation to your class that includes two things: an introduction to the plot and the characters, and an introduction to some of the melodies that the students can listen for, that are associated with certain characters, things, ideas, or events, especially if those melodies can be heard in many places throughout the opera.
- If the opera company cannot send someone, you may still be able to find a local musician or music teacher (or college student!) who can make this presentation to your class. If not, you may be able

---

[53]"What Kind of Music is That?" <http://cnx.org/content/m11421/latest/#p3aa>

to make it yourself using program notes from a recording of the opera. A text on opera such as *The Definitive Kobbe's Opera Book* can also be helpful in this regard, particularly if you play piano and can play the themes and motifs in it for your class.

Procedure

- Introduce the students to some of the motifs or musical themes of the opera, before they attend the performance. Recognizing the motifs (and knowing what they represent) can make the performance much more involving.
- The procedure for familiarizing the students with the motifs will depend on the resources you have found. Try to ensure that the students recognize at least the main motifs, whenever they hear them, and know what each represents, before they attend the performance. Tell them what the discussion points will be after the performance.
- Attend the performance, or watch the recording.
- Follow the performance with a short discussion. Which motifs did the students notice the most? When did they hear them? (Who was on stage; who was singing; what was happening in the plot?) What was the connection with the character or plot?
- You may also follow the discussion with an assignment to write an essay about the performance. Besides a discussion of the use of motifs, subjects for the essay could include a synopsis and/or analysis of the plot, a discussion of the characters or of the musical style, or a research paper on the composer or the time period.

2.2.5.4 Composing and Improvising using Motifs

Objectives and Assessment

- **Grade Level** - 6-12
- **Student Prerequisites** - Students must have have some experience playing instruments, and must be able to write common notation[54] fairly accurately.
- **Teacher Expertise** - The teacher should be trained in basic performance, composition, and/or improvisation techniques.
- **Time Requirements** - Depending on the circumstances, you may make this an individual homework assignment, and then have the students play their compositions for each other during class time; or, this can be an in-class group activity. Amount of time necessary depends on student facility in composition and improvisation, and on number of student or group performances.
- **Objectives** - The student will compose, manipulate and use motifs in composition an/or improvisation.
- **Evaluation** - For assessment, look at melodic and rhythmic quality of motif, ability to manipulate the motif in more than one way, and successful use of the motif in the composition or improvisation.

Materials and Preparation

- Every student will need access to a musical instrument that they can play comfortably. (Or, if this is a group project, one instrument and player per group is sufficient. If the entire class is composing as a group, the teacher may be the player.) Blank staff paper and pencils with erasers will also be needed.
- If this is an in-class activity, each group will need an individual space (or time), so they can hear their own ideas being played. If this is not possible, do the activity as a full-class group, with students taking turns or cooperating in humming or singing ideas to be played and written down by others.
- If there is not sufficient "quiet space" in the classroom, and the students have access to instruments at home or outside of class time, make this an individual homework assignment.

Procedure

---

[54]"The Staff" <http://cnx.org/content/m10880/latest/>

- Each student or group will first write a short melodic motif.
- Each student or group should then experiment with the motif, finding several different expressions of it (in a different key[55], for example, or using different intervals[56] or rhythms (Section 1.1), or playing the motif "backwards" or "upside-down") that are pleasant and still recognizable as that motif.
- Each student or group will compose a short instrumental piece, using at least three of the different expressions of the motif to make a melody that is unified but interesting. (They may use each variation of the motif as many times as they want.)
- If the students are learning how to improvise, they may also be given an opportunity to improvise using motifs. Unless the students are already confident improvisers, they will still benefit from the exercise of writing out and practicing a motif and its possible variations before being asked to improvise using that motif (and its variations). If the students are learning to improvise over changes, have them identify which variations of the motif might work with particular chords before they try to improvise. If they are beginning improvisers, ask them to improvise their motif-based melody without a harmonic background, or give them the changes and allow them to compose and memorize at least one motif-based melody that works with the changes before trying to improvise (with the same motif) over the changes.

2.3 Harmony

2.3.1 Harmony[57]

When you have more than one pitch[58] sounding at the same time in music, the result is **harmony**. Harmony is one of the basic elements of music, but it is not as basic as some other elements, such as rhythm (Section 1.1) and melody (Section 2.2.1). You can have music that is just rhythms, with no pitches at all. You can also have music that is just a single melody, or just a melody with rhythm accompaniment (Accompaniment, p. 54).

But as soon as there is more than one pitch sounding at a time, you have harmony. Even if nobody is actually playing chords (Chords, p. 53), or even if the notes are part of independent contrapuntal (Section 3.3) lines, you can hear the relationship of any notes that happen at the same time, and it is this relationship that makes the harmony.

> NOTE: Harmony does not have to be particularly "harmonious"; it may be quite dissonant[59], in fact. For the purpose of definitions, the important fact is the notes sounding at the same time.

Harmony is the most emphasized and most highly developed element in Western music[60], and can be the subject of an entire course on music theory. Many of the concepts underlying Western harmony are explained in greater detail elsewhere (see Triads[61] and Beginning Harmonic Analysis[62], for example), but here are some basic terms and short definitions that you may find useful in discussions of harmony:

Harmony Textures

- **implied harmony** - A melody all by itself (Monophony (Section 3.1.2: Terms that Describe Texture)) can have an implied harmony, even if no other notes are sounding at the same time. In other words, the melody can be constructed so that it strongly suggests a harmony that could accompany it. For example, when you sing a melody by itself, you may be able to "hear" in your mind the chords that

---

[55]"Major Keys and Scales" <http://cnx.org/content/m10851/latest/>
[56]"Interval" <http://cnx.org/content/m10867/latest/>
[57]This content is available online at <http://cnx.org/content/m11654/1.7/>.
[58]"Pitch: Sharp, Flat, and Natural Notes" <http://cnx.org/content/m10943/latest/>
[59]"Consonance and Dissonance" <http://cnx.org/content/m11953/latest/>
[60]"What Kind of Music is That?" <http://cnx.org/content/m11421/latest/>
[61]"Triads" <http://cnx.org/content/m10877/latest/>
[62]"Beginning Harmonic Analysis" <http://cnx.org/content/m11643/latest/>

usually go with it. A Bach unaccompanied cello suite also has strongly implied harmonies; if someone really wanted to play an accompaniment (Accompaniment, p. 54), the appropriate chords (Chords, p. 53) could be found pretty easily. But some melodies don't imply any harmony; they are not meant to be played with harmony, and don't need it to be legitimate music. (Good examples of this include plainchant, some modern art music, and some Non-Western[63] music, for example, Native American flute music.)

- **drones** - The simplest way to add harmony to a melody is to play it with drones. A drone is a note that changes rarely or not at all. Drones can be most easily found in bagpipes music, Indian Classical[64] music and other musics that use instruments that traditionally play drone notes. (See Harmony with Drones (Section 2.3.2).)
- **parallel harmony** - Parallel harmony occurs when different lines in the music go up or down together (usually following the melody). (See Parallel Harmonies (Section 2.3.4) for examples.)
- **homophony** - Homophony is a texture (Section 3.1) of music in which there is one line that is obviously the melody. The rest of the notes are harmony and accompaniment (Accompaniment, p. 54). (See Homophonic (Section 3.1.2.2: Homophonic).)
- **polyphony** or **counterpoint** - Both of these terms refer to a texture of music in which there is more than one independent melodic line at the same time, and they are all fairly equal in importance. (See Polyphonic (Section 3.1.2.3: Polyphonic) and Counterpoint (Section 3.3).)

Chords

- **chords** - In Western[65] music, most harmony is based on chords. **Chords** are groups of notes built on major[66] or minor[67] triads[68]. In traditional triadic harmony, there are always at least three notes in a chord (there can be more than three), but some of the notes may be left out and only "implied" by the harmony. The notes of the chord may be played at the same time (**block chords**), or may be played separately with some overlap, or may be played separately but in a quick enough succession that they will be "heard" as a chord or understood to imply a chord (**arpeggiated chords** or **arpeggios**).
- **chord progression** - A series of chords played one after another is a chord progression. Musicians may describe a specific chord progression (for example, "two measures of G major, then a half measure of A minor and a half measure of D seventh", or just "G, A minor, D seventh") or speak more generally of classes of chord progressions (for example a "blues chord progression"). Please see Beginning Harmonic Analysis[69] for more information.

Harmonic Analysis

- **harmonic rhythm** - The harmonic rhythm of a piece refers to how often the chords change. Music in which the chords change rarely has a slow harmonic rhythm; music in which the chords change often has a fast harmonic rhythm. Harmonic rhythm can be completely separate from other rhythms and tempos. For example, a section of music with many short, quick notes but only one chord has fast rhythms but a slow harmonic rhythm.
- **cadence** - A cadence is a point where the music feels as if it has come to a temporary or permanent stopping point. In most Western[70] music, cadence is tied very strongly to the harmony. For example, most listeners will feel that the strongest, most satisfying ending to a piece of music involves a dominant chord[71] followed by a tonic chord[72]. In fact, a song that does not end on the tonic chord will sound

---

[63] "What Kind of Music is That?" <http://cnx.org/content/m11421/latest/>
[64] "Listening to Indian Classical Music" <http://cnx.org/content/m12502/latest/>
[65] "What Kind of Music is That?" <http://cnx.org/content/m11421/latest/>
[66] "Major Keys and Scales" <http://cnx.org/content/m10851/latest/>
[67] "Minor Keys and Scales" <http://cnx.org/content/m10856/latest/>
[68] "Triads" <http://cnx.org/content/m10877/latest/>
[69] "Beginning Harmonic Analysis" <http://cnx.org/content/m11643/latest/>
[70] "What Kind of Music is That?" <http://cnx.org/content/m11421/latest/>
[71] "Beginning Harmonic Analysis": Section Naming Chords Within a Key <http://cnx.org/content/m11643/latest/#s3>
[72] "Beginning Harmonic Analysis": Section Naming Chords Within a Key <http://cnx.org/content/m11643/latest/#s3>

quite unsettled and even unfinished to most listeners. (See Cadence[73].)

- **diatonic** - Diatonic[74] harmony stays in a particular major[75] or minor[76] key.
- **chromatic** - Chromatic[77] harmony includes many notes and chords that are not in the key and so contains many accidentals[78].
- **dissonance** - A dissonance is a note, chord, or interval[79] that does not fit into the triadic[80] harmonies that we have learned to expect from music. A dissonance may sound surprising, jarring, even unpleasant.

Accompaniment

- **accompaniment** - All the parts of the music that are not melody are part of the accompaniment. This includes rhythmic parts, harmonies, the bass line, and chords.
- **melodic line** - This is just another term for the string of notes that make up the melody (Section 2.2.1).
- **bass line** - The bass line is the string of notes that are the lowest notes being sung or played. Because of basic laws of physics, the bass line sets up the harmonics[81] that all the other parts - including the melody - must fit into. This makes it a very important line both for tuning[82] and for the harmony. The bass line also often outlines the chord progression (Chords, p. 53), and it is often the most noticeable line of the accompaniment.
- **inner parts** or **inner voices** - Accompaniment parts that fill in the music in between the melody (which is often the highest part) and the bass line.
- **descant** - The melody is not always the highest line in the music. Attention is naturally drawn to high notes, so a part that is higher than the melody is sometimes given a special name such as "descant". This term is an old one going all the way back to when harmonies first began to be added to medieval chant. (See Counterpoint (p. 72) for more about descants.)

Suggestions for activities that introduce young students to harmony may be found in Harmony with Drones (Section 2.3.2), Simple Chordal Harmony (Section 2.3.3), Parallel Harmonies (Section 2.3.4), and Independent Harmonies (Section 2.3.5).

2.3.2 Harmony with Drones[83]

Materials and Preparation

- If you can, find a recording of music that uses drones and a CD or tape player to play it for the class. Bagpipe music or classical music from India will probably be the easiest to find, but some more uncommon instruments from various music traditions, like the Appalachian dulcimer (not the hammered dulcimer) may also have drones.
- Decide on a song to teach your students that has a drone part in the voice or on instruments. Use "Sarasponda" if you like.
- If it would be helpful, have copies of the song for the students.
- Be ready to teach the students the melody and the drone part(s). Here is the melody to Sarasponda with[84] and without[85] the drone part.

---

[73]"Cadence in Music" <http://cnx.org/content/m12402/latest/>
[74]"What Kind of Music is That?" <http://cnx.org/content/m11421/latest/#p7f>
[75]"Major Keys and Scales" <http://cnx.org/content/m10851/latest/>
[76]"Minor Keys and Scales" <http://cnx.org/content/m10856/latest/>
[77]"What Kind of Music is That?" <http://cnx.org/content/m11421/latest/#p7f>
[78]"Pitch: Sharp, Flat, and Natural Notes" <http://cnx.org/content/m10943/latest/#p0e>
[79]"Interval" <http://cnx.org/content/m10867/latest/>
[80]"Triads" <http://cnx.org/content/m10877/latest/>
[81]"Harmonic Series I: Timbre and Octaves" <http://cnx.org/content/m13682/latest/>
[82]"Tuning Systems" <http://cnx.org/content/m11639/latest/>
[83]This content is available online at <http://cnx.org/content/m11844/1.1/>.
[84]http://cnx.org/content/m11844/latest/saraspondaw.mid
[85]http://cnx.org/content/m11844/latest/saraspondawo.mid

- If the drone is on an instrument, have instruments for at least several students to play.

Sarasponda

Drone during verse:

Boom-da, boom-da, boom-da, boom-da,

Verse:

Sa- ra- spon- da, sa- ra- spon- da, sa- ra- spon- da, ret- set- set! Sa- ra-

spon- da, sa- ra- spon- da, sa- ra- spon- da, ret- set- set!

Refrain (all together):

Ah- do- day- oh!   Ah- do- ray- boom- day- oh!   Ah-

do- ray- boom- day- ret- set- set!   Ah- say- pah- say- oh!

Figure 2.10

Procedure

1. Explain to your students that a **drone** is the simplest kind of harmony. The melody is played along with one or two notes that never (or very rarely) change.
2. Play your example recording for them. Can they identify the drone notes by humming or singing them along with the instruments?
3. Hand out the copies of the song you are going to teach them. Teach them all the melody, going over it as many times as necessary until they are confident.
4. Now teach them the drone part and let a small part of the class sing or play the drone part while the rest sing the melody again. Let them all take a turn with the drone.

2.3.3 Simple Chordal Harmony[86]

2.3.3.1 Introduction

One simple way to provide harmony for a melody is to add chords (Chords, p. 53). The notes of each chord may be played all at once (**block chords**), or they may be played one at a time (**broken** or **arpeggiated** chords). For example, a person playing a guitar can strum the chord (this would be a "block" chord) or use a picking style to play "broken" chords. As long as the accompaniment is just chords, and not a different melody, it still belongs in this category of simple chordal accompaniment. Another very common way to play simple chordal accompaniments is to alternate playing the bass note of the chord and the rest of the chord. This is the "oom-pah-oom-pah" (bass-chord-bass-chord) or "oom-pah-pah-oom-pah-pah" (bass-chord-chord-bass-chord-chord) that you often hear pianos or bands playing.

This kind of harmony is unusual in classical music and also in professionally produced popular musics, but it is very common in Western[87] music wherever people are making music for their own enjoyment: folk musics, sing-alongs, informal dances, children's music, some styles of sacred music, and amateurs playing pop music for fun. One of the features of Western music, in fact, is instruments that easily play this kind of accompaniment. The many keyboard instruments, guitar, banjo, lute, accordions, and dulcimers are some of the more common, but there are plenty of uncommon ones, too. (Can you or your students name any?)

2.3.3.2 Activities

Materials and Preparation

- Find an audio player and some recordings of music that is melody with only chordal accompaniment. You will find some suggestion at the end of the lesson.
- Have the tapes ready to play at the right spot, or know CD track numbers.
- Choose a song for the class to sing with chordal accompaniment. You (or someone) can accompany them with simple or arpeggiated chords on keyboard or guitar, or you can teach them to sing the chords. If they are going to sing the accompaniment, choose a song with few chord changes, unless you and they are up to a challenge. (If you are looking for a challenge, they might enjoy learning "The Lion Sleeps Tonight"; the "wi-mo-wep" part is just rhythmical chords.) If you want to try something pretty simple, you may use "She'll Be Comin' Round the Mountain". You can play (or have someone else play) the chords on an instrument, or you can have some of the students sing the chords with "oohs".
- If your students would find it useful, have plenty of copies for them of the song you have chosen.
- If someone is going to play an accompaniment, you will need your accompanist and instrument. If the students are going to sing the song you have chosen, you may need a pitchpipe or keyboard to give them their beginning notes.

---

[86] This content is available online at <http://cnx.org/content/m11875/1.2/>.
[87] "What Kind of Music is That?" <http://cnx.org/content/m11421/latest/>

(a) She'll be Comin' Round the Mountain

(b)

Figure 2.11: If you need to hear any of the parts, here are the melody alone[88], the high whoos[89], the middle whoos[90], the low whoos[91], all the whoos together[92], and all the whoos with the melody[93]. All parts start on the same note, so that you do not need a pitchpipe or musical instrument to give all the parts their beginning notes. They do not necessarily even have to start on a D; just start them all out on the same (reasonably low) note. (a) The students can be accompanied by a piano, guitar, banjo, accordion, autoharp, or dulcimer, playing the chords (in red) in whatever manner suits the instrument and player. Or you may have some students sing the melody, while some sing the chords. If each "woo" chord begins with a slight dip, the effect will be a little like a train whistle.

Procedure

1. Explain that one of the easiest ways to add harmony to a melody is to simply play (or sing) the chords along with it.
2. Play your chosen recorded examples for the class. Explain that the notes of the chords may be played one at a time; as long as the accompaniment is just broken up chords and not another melody, it is still just a simple chordal harmony.
3. If you have them, hand out copies of the song they are going to learn.
4. Teach the entire class the melody.
5. If you are or have an accompanist, have them sing the melody again, first with the accompanist playing block chords, then again with a simple chord-based accompaniment.

[88] http://cnx.org/content/m11875/latest/cominroundmel.mid
[89] http://cnx.org/content/m11875/latest/cominround1.MID
[90] http://cnx.org/content/m11875/latest/cominround2.MID
[91] http://cnx.org/content/m11875/latest/cominround3.MID
[92] http://cnx.org/content/m11875/latest/cominroundchord.MID
[93] http://cnx.org/content/m11875/latest/cominroundall.MID

6. If they are going to sing the accompaniment, assign each student a part (low, middle, or high note of the chord), and teach them the part. Once they can sing just the chords together, leave half of them on the chords and let the other half sing the melody. Then let everyone switch parts.

2.3.3.3 Listening Suggestions

As mentioned above, most professionally produced recordings, whether popular, jazz, or classical, feature more complex accompaniments. Here are some places to look for this simple musical texture (Section 3.1).

- Two classical works that do feature this texture are "The March of the Toreadors" from Bizet's *Carmen* and the familiar "graduation march" tune from Elgar's *Pomp and Circumstance #1*. (If you do look up a recording of the Elgar piece, it is not the beginning of the piece that you want to listen to; the familiar tune comes later on).
- Consider arranging for a live performance for your class. Ask anyone who plays guitar or piano competently for a demonstration of simple chordal accompaniments. They may be willing to provide the melody also, on their instrument or vocally, or they may be able to provide a soloist or may ask the class to help by singing the melody.
- Recordings that are meant for children, the many "Wee Sing" tapes, for example, often feature simple chordal accompaniments.
- Many folk artists and blues artists who perform solo (Joan Baez or Odetta, for example) have made recordings in this style.
- Some solo piano music (Chopin's Prelude No. 4 in E minor or Nocturne No. 2 in E flat, for example) and solo classical guitar (the "Granada" movement of Albeniz' *Suite Espanola*, for example).
- Some classic ragtime, like Joplin's "Maple Leaf Rag" feature a simple "oom-pah" acompaniment.

2.3.4 Parallel Harmonies[94]

Parallel harmony is harmony that generally follows the melody, going up when the melody goes up and down when the melody goes down. Because parallel harmonies are not independent of the melody, they do not follow the rules of well-written counterpoint (Section 3.3) and are generally not considered to be as interesting as independent harmony parts (Section 2.3.5). However, parallel harmonies are easier to play for many instruments (keyboard instruments, guitar, dobro guitar, violin, and cello, to name just a few). Parallel harmonies are also very easy for even the "untrained ear" to grasp, and are very common in popular and folk musics. In Western classical[95] music, they are most common in Impressionist music and in some types of medieval chant.

Materials and Preparation

- You will need some recordings with easy-to-hear parallel harmonies and a tape or CD player to play them on.
- Have your chosen tapes ready to play at the correct spot, or know the CD track numbers.
- Choose a song with a parallel harmony for them to learn. Some Christmas songs, such as "Away in a Manger" and "Silent Night", have well-known parallel harmonies, as do many popular and folk tunes. Look for harmony parts that seem to follow closely the contour (Section 2.2.1.2: The Shape or Contour of a Melody) of the melody. If you would like, you can use "America, the Beautiful", below.
- If it would help your students, have copies of the words, or the words and music, of your chosen song available for them.
- You can plan for the students to sing the song without accompaniment, or accompany them yourself, or arrange for an accompanist.

---

[94] This content is available online at <http://cnx.org/content/m11878/1.1/>.
[95] "What Kind of Music is That?" <http://cnx.org/content/m11421/latest/>

Listening Suggestions: There's plenty of parallel harmony to be heard in:

- some ragtime tunes, such as Scott Joplin's "The Entertainer".
- many popular "Country" music songs and modern Hawaiian pop tunes, especially in the vocals and in the dobro guitar parts, and in some folk styles (listen to the group Ladysmith Black Mambazo, for example).
- many pieces for solo violin, such as Brahms' Hungarian dances (listen, for example, to the slow sections of "Hungarian Dance No. 4 in Bm").
- the saxes and brass in some Big Band jazz tunes such as "String of Pearls" and "In the Mood".
- here and there in symphonic music; for example listen to the flutes in the "Dance of the Mirlitons" in Tchaikovsky's *The Nutcracker*, or in the "Gypsy Song" from Bizet's *Carmen*.

Procedure

1. Explain to your students that one kind of harmony that you can add to music is called **parallel harmony**. This is more complex and interesting than drones (Section 2.3.2) but less complex and interesting than independent harmony (Section 2.3.5).
2. If they have covered the term **parallel** in math, remind them of this. If they have not, tell them that in math, parallel lines are lines that are going in exactly the same direction, so that they seem to follow each other and yet never meet or cross each other. The two long sides of a ruler are a good example.
3. Explain that in music, parallel harmonies are harmony lines that go in the same direction as the melody. When the melody goes up, so does the harmony. When the melody goes down, so does the harmony. But the rules for musical parallels aren't as strict as the rules for mathematical parallels. Parallel harmonies don't have to always move in the same direction as the melody by exactly the same amount. In fact, because they need to fit in with the chords and also provide some interest, parallel harmonies are usually not exactly parallel all the time. They can even meet or cross the melody sometimes.
4. Play your chosen recordings, pointing out the places where parallel harmonies are most easily heard.
5. If you have copies of the song for the students, hand them out.
6. Depending on your class logistics, you may teach all the students both the melody and the harmony, or you may divide the class up and teach each group only one part. It may take several sessions for both groups to be able to sing their parts with enough confidence. It often works best to have more students on the melody, but some of the stronger singers on the harmony.

Figure 2.12: If you need to, you can listen to the melody[96], harmony[97], and both together[98].

2.3.5 Independent Harmonies[99]

2.3.5.1 Introduction

A harmony is independent of the melody (Section 2.2.1) if it is often doing something different from the melody. Even if it is not independent enough to be counterpoint, such harmony adds more depth and interest to the music than drones (Section 2.3.2), parallel harmonies (Section 2.3.4), or simple chordal accompaniments (Section 2.3.3). So this type of harmony is extremely popular for hymns and other choral arrangements, and it is also very common in instrumental music and in instrumental accompaniments.

What makes a harmony or accompaniment part independent?

- If it often has different rhythms than the melody, it is independent.

---

[96] http://cnx.org/content/m11878/latest/americamel.mid
[97] http://cnx.org/content/m11878/latest/americaharm.mid
[98] http://cnx.org/content/m11878/latest/americaboth.mid
[99] This content is available online at <http://cnx.org/content/m11874/1.2/>.

- Even if it has the same rhythms as the melody, it is independent if it is often moving in a different direction from the melody; for example, the harmony part is going down when the melody is going up.
- If a harmony is truly independent, then even when it is moving in the same direction as the melody, it is usually moving by a different interval[100]. For example, if the melody is going up by perfect fourth[101], it might go up by a single half step[102].

Independent harmonies are not quite counterpoint (Section 3.3). In order to be considered true counterpoint or polyphony (Section 3.1.2.3: Polyphonic), the different parts must be not only independent, they must also sound like equally important melodies. Is there always a very clear line between independent harmony and counterpoint? No! Remember that all of the rules and definitions in music theory ("counterpoint", "harmony", "minor keys") were all made up to describe what good composers were already doing; they do not define what a composer is allowed to do. If the composer - or performer - likes, an independent line can easily drift back and forth between being a background, harmony part, and being so important that it becomes a countermelody (Section 3.3.2: Some Useful Terms).

But in much classical and popular music, there is one line that is clearly the melody. The harmonies or accompaniment parts are all clearly "background", but they still follow most of the important rules of counterpoint. **The most important rule of counterpoint is that two lines should not move in parallel.** In other words, when the melody goes down one step, the harmony should do something other than going down one step; it can go down by a different interval[103], or stay the same, but it is best if it goes up. When the melody goes up a perfect fourth, the harmony should do anything other than go up a perfect fourth. Independent harmonies also follow this rule.

For much homophonic music (Section 3.1.2.2: Homophonic), following this basic rule about contrasting intervals[104] is enough. In particular, there is a great deal of choral music (most traditional Western[105] hymns, for example) in which all the parts have different intervals but use the same rhythms, so that everybody is singing the same word at the same time. This type of texture is sometimes called **homorhythmic**.

Other harmony or accompaniment parts are even more independent, and have a different rhythm from the melody also. Good examples of this are the bass line in most pop songs or the instrumental parts accompanying an opera aria. In these types of music, as well as in much jazz and symphonic music, there is one line that is clearly the melody, but the other parts aren't simply following along with the melody. They are "doing their own thing".

2.3.5.2 Activities

Materials and Preparation

- You will need an audiotape or CD player.
- Choose some music with independent harmonies for your students to listen to. (There are some suggestions below (Suggested Listening List, p. 63).) If you have the class time for it, and you have not already covered monody (Section 3.1.2: Terms that Describe Texture), drones (Section 2.3.2), chordal harmonies (Section 2.3.3), and parallel harmonies (Section 2.3.4), you may want to include some examples of these for contrast. Suggested recordings for these other textures can be found in those lessons.)
- Choose a song with independent harmonies for them to learn. Since this is fairly challenging, keep it simple unless you have older, musically trained students. If your students are up to the challenge, this type of harmony is not difficult to find; most SATB choral arrangements feature independent harmonies. If you would like a very simple example for young or musically inexperienced students, or if you are not experienced enough to tackle full-fledged harmonies, you may use "Train is a-Comin'",

---

[100]"Interval" <http://cnx.org/content/m10867/latest/>
[101]"Interval": Section Perfect Intervals <http://cnx.org/content/m10867/latest/#s21>
[102]"Half Steps and Whole Steps" <http://cnx.org/content/m10866/latest/>
[103]"Interval" <http://cnx.org/content/m10867/latest/>
[104]"Interval" <http://cnx.org/content/m10867/latest/>
[105]"What Kind of Music is That?" <http://cnx.org/content/m11421/latest/>

below. In this version, much of the song is in unison, with simple (but independent) harmonies in only a few places in the music. If you need to, listen to the melody[106], higher harmony[107], and lower harmony[108], and all the parts together[109].

- If you would like, arrange for an accompanist. An accompanist is not necessary for this style of singing (not even for a simple piece like "Train is a-Comin'"), but it may make things much easier or more comfortable for the singers.
- Have enough copies of the words and music for the students.

Train is a-Comin'

Figure 2.13: The notes in black are the melody. Red notes are an extensive high harmony; give this to a few students who are ready for a challenge. Blue notes are a very small low harmony part, which can be ignored if you like; if you have a few more students who can sing a few notes that are not in the melody, give this part to them. Everyone should sing the melody whenever they do not have a harmony part.

---

[106] http://cnx.org/content/m11874/latest/traincominmel.mid
[107] http://cnx.org/content/m11874/latest/traincominhigh.mid
[108] http://cnx.org/content/m11874/latest/traincominlow.mid
[109] http://cnx.org/content/m11874/latest/traincominall.mid

Procedure

1. Using the introduction above (p. 60) as a guide, talk with the class about independent harmonies. Introduce any definitions you want them to learn, and contrast this musical texture with any other textures you have studied or will study, including monody (Section 3.1.2: Terms that Describe Texture), drones (Section 2.3.2), parallel harmonies (Section 2.3.4), chordal harmonies (Section 2.3.3), and counterpoint (Section 3.3).
2. Play some of your examples of music with independent harmonies or accompaniment. Ask the students to hum along with the melody the first time. Play the example again. Can they hum along with the bass line or another harmony or accompaniment part the second time? How different are the parts?
3. If you have them, play some of your examples of monody, drones, parallel harmony, chordal accompaniment, and counterpoint, for contrast. If you have also studied these other textures, identify them as they are listening to them.
4. If you have enough examples, play some more, asking the students to identify the pieces with independent harmonies. Can they identify the other textures as well?
5. Divide the students into higher and lower voices and assign appropriate parts for the song they will sing.
6. Teach each group its part (this may be done over the course of several sessions) and have them practice it alone before attempting to combine the groups.

The suggestions for recordings to look for are pretty vague because there is so much music in this category. It is very easy to find, so you should not spend a lot of time looking for specific recordings. Just make sure there is one clear and obvious melody in your selections, but that the accompaniment to it is interesting and independent of the melody. The choral selections will be more likely to be homorhythmic (p. 61), so that the words can be easily understood, whereas instrumental accompaniments will tend to be even more independent.

Suggested Listening List

- Almost any chorus from a Gilbert and Sullivan opera.
- Recordings of choirs singing traditional (nineteenth-century) hymns.
- If you have trouble hearing hymn harmonies, try listening to the chorales of Bach's *Christmas Oratorio (Weinachts Oratorium)*. The chorales are not contrapuntal - the melody is clearly in the soprano part, and the different parts sing the same words at the same time - but it is unusually easy to hear that the parts are in fact quite different from each other.
- Pop music with a solo singer, a strong bass line, and interesting instrumental accompaniment.
- Most opera arias and many opera choruses.
- This is also one of the most common textures (Section 3.1) in orchestral music, particularly in classical-era and Romantic-era symphonies (Mozart, Haydn, Beethoven, Schubert, etc.) But be aware that in symphonic music, texture can change often and quickly.

Chapter 3

Combining Time and Pitch

3.1 The Textures of Music[1]

3.1.1 Introduction

Texture is one of the basic elements of music. When you describe the **texture** of a piece of music, you are describing how much is going on in the music at any given moment. For example, the texture of the music might be thick or thin, or it may have many or few layers. It might be made up of rhythm only, or of a melody line with chordal accompaniment, or many interweaving melodies. Below you will find some of the formal terms musicians use to describe texture. Suggestions for activities to introduce the concept of texture to young students can be found in Musical Textures Activities (Section 3.2).

3.1.2 Terms that Describe Texture

There are many informal terms that can describe the texture of a piece of music (thick, thin, bass-heavy, rhythmically complex, and so on), but the formal terms that are used to describe texture all describe the relationships of melodies (Section 2.2.1) and harmonies (Section 2.3.1). Here are definitions and examples of the four main types of texture. For specific pieces of music that are good examples of each type of texture, please see below (Section 3.1.3: Suggested Listening).

3.1.2.1 Monophonic

Monophonic music has only one melodic (Section 2.2.1) line, with no harmony (Section 2.3.1) or counterpoint (Section 3.3). There may be rhythmic (Section 1.1) accompaniment, but only one line that has specific pitches[2]. Monophonic music can also be called **monophony**. It is sometimes called **monody**, although the term "monody" can also refer to a particular type of solo song (with instrumental accompaniment) that was very popular in the 1600's.

Examples of Monophony

- One person whistling a tune
- A single bugle sounding "Taps"
- A group of people all singing a song together, without harmonies or instruments
- A fife and drum corp, with all the fifes playing the same melody

---

[1]This content is available online at <http://cnx.org/content/m11645/1.7/>.
[2]"Pitch: Sharp, Flat, and Natural Notes" <http://cnx.org/content/m10943/latest/>

3.1.2.2 Homophonic

Homophonic music can also be called **homophony**. More informally, people who are describing homophonic music may mention chords (Chords, p. 53), accompaniment (Accompaniment, p. 54), harmony or harmonies (Section 2.3.1). Homophony has one clearly melodic (Section 2.2.1) line; it's the line that naturally draws your attention. All other parts provide accompaniment or fill in the chords. In most well-written homophony, the parts that are not melody may still have a lot of melodic interest. They may follow many of the rules of well-written counterpoint (Section 3.3), and they can sound quite different from the melody and be interesting to listen to by themselves. But when they are sung or played with the melody, it is clear that they are not independent melodic parts, either because they have the same rhythm as the melody (i.e. are not independent) or because their main purpose is to fill in the chords or harmony (i.e. they are not really melodies).

Examples of Homophony

- Choral music in which the parts have mostly the same rhythms at the same time is homophonic. Most traditional Protestant hymns and most "barbershop quartet" music is in this category.
- A singer accompanied by a guitar picking or strumming chords.
- A small jazz combo with a bass, a piano, and a drum set providing the "rhythm" background for a trumpet improvising a solo.
- A single bagpipes or accordion player playing a melody with drones or chords.

3.1.2.3 Polyphonic

Polyphonic music can also be called **polyphony**, **counterpoint**, or **contrapuntal** music. If more than one independent melody (Section 2.2.1) is occurring at the same time, the music is polyphonic. (See counterpoint (Section 3.3).)

Examples of Polyphony

- Rounds, canons, and fugues (Section 3.3.2: Some Useful Terms) are all polyphonic. (Even if there is only one melody, if different people are singing or playing it at different times, the parts sound independent.)
- Much Baroque music is contrapuntal, particularly the works of J.S. Bach.
- Most music for large instrumental groups such as bands or orchestras is contrapuntal at least some of the time.
- Music that is mostly homophonic can become temporarily polyphonic if an independent countermelody is added. Think of a favorite pop or gospel tune that, near the end, has the soloist "ad libbing" while the back-up singers repeat the refrain.

3.1.2.4 Heterophonic

A **heterophonic** texture is rare in Western[3] music. In **heterophony**, there is only one melody, but different variations of it are being sung or played at the same time.

- Heterophony can be heard in the Bluegrass, "mountain music", Cajun, and Zydeco traditions. Listen for the tune to be played by two instruments (say fiddle and banjo) at the same time, with each adding the embellishments, ornaments (Section 2.2.1), and flourishes that are characteristic of the instrument.
- Some Middle Eastern, South Asian, central Eurasian, and Native American music traditions include heterophony. Listen for traditional music (most modern-composed music, even from these cultures, has little or no heterophony) in which singers and/or instrumentalists perform the same melody at the same time, but give it different embellishments or ornaments.

---

[3]"What Kind of Music is That?" <http://cnx.org/content/m11421/latest/>

3.1.3 Suggested Listening

Monophony

- Here is an excerpt[4] from James Romig's[5] Sonnet 2, played by John McMurtery.
- A Bach unaccompanied cello suite
- Gregorian chant
- Long sections of "The People that Walked in Darkness" aria in Handel's "Messiah" are monophonic (the instruments are playing the same line as the voice). Apparently Handel associates monophony with "walking in darkness"!

Homophony

- A classic Scott Joplin rag such as "Maple Leaf Rag" or "The Entertainer"
- The "graduation march" section of Edward Elgar's "Pomp and Circumstance No. 1"
- The "March of the Toreadors" from Bizet's *Carmen*
- No. 1 ("Granada") of Albeniz' Suite Espanola for guitar
- The latest hit tune by a major pop solo vocalist
- The opening section of the "Overture" Of Handel's "Messiah" (The second section of the overture is polyphonic)

Polyphony

- Pachelbel's Canon
- Anything titled "fugue" or "invention"
- The final "Amen" chorus of Handel's "Messiah"
- The trio strain of Sousa's "Stars and Stripes Forever", with the famous piccolo countermelody
- The "One Day More" chorus from the musical "Les Miserables"
- The first movement of Holst's 1st Suite for Military Band

Heterophony

- There is some heterophony (with some instruments playing more ornaments than others) in "Donulmez Aksamin" and in "Urfaliyim Ezelden" on the Turkish Music[6] page.
- The performance of "Lonesome Valley" by the Fairfield Four on the "O Brother, Where Art Thou" soundtrack is quite heterophonic. (Old-style blues owes more to African than to Western traditions.)

3.2 A Musical Textures Activity[7]

For an explanation of musical texture terms, please see The Textures of Music (Section 3.1). Below are a classroom activity that will familiarize your students with any of the texture terms you want them to know, and a list of suggested musical examples (Section 3.2.1: Suggested Music) of each texture.

Goals and Assessment

- **Goals** - The student will learn to recognize different musical textures when presented aurally, and to use appropriate terminology in discussing texture in music.
- **Grade Level** - K-12
- **Student Prerequisites** - none

---

[4] http://cnx.org/content/m11645/latest/sonnet2exc.mp3
[5] http://www.jamesromig.com
[6] http://www.focusmm.com/turkey/tr_musmn.htm
[7] This content is available online at <http://cnx.org/content/m14260/1.4/>.

- **Teacher Expertise** - Teacher expertise in music education is not necessary to present this activity. The teacher should be familiar and comfortable with the terms and concepts regarding musical texture (Section 3.1), and, when listening to music, should be able to identify the texture.
- **Time Requirements** - All four textures may be presented in one (approximately 45-minute) class period. You may prefer to break the activity up and present it in several 10-15-minute sessions, with each session reviewing previously-learned textures and introducing one new texture. The final session can then be a short reminder-review and listening test.
- **Music Standards Addressed** - National Standards for Music Education[8] standard 6 (listening to, analyzing, and describing music). If several of your musical examples are from other cultures or time periods, this activity also addresses standard 9 (understanding music in relation to history and culture).
- **Objectives** - For each musical texture studied, the student will listen to several clear examples of the texture and learn the appropriate terms to describe it. Listening to several new "mystery" excerpts, the student will determine whether it is or is not an example of the texture being studied. Finally, the student will listen to several more "mystery" excerpts and correctly name the texture heard.
- **Evaluation** - Assess student learning by grading the completed worksheet or noting accuracy of verbal answers.
- **Follow-up** - To help these concepts enter long-term memory, continue to talk about the "texture" of musical pieces throughout the rest of the year. Ask students to identify the texture of a new piece they are learning to sing or play, or discuss the tendency of music from particular cultures or time periods to be one texture or another.

Materials and Preparation

- You will need a CD or tape player.
- Gather music recordings that illustrate each texture you would like to cover. Use the suggestion list below (Section 3.2.1: Suggested Music), or make your own choices based on your music library and students' preferences.
- Know the track number for each of your examples, or have the tape ready to play at the right spot.
- If you wish, make copies of this hand-out for your students. The handout is available as a PDF file[9]. It is also included here as a figure, but the PDF file will make a nicer-looking handout. You can cover up or black out any terms you will not be covering. Or, instead of using the handout, write the terms on the board for them.

---

[8] http://menc.org/resources/view/national-standards-for-music-education
[9] http://cnx.org/content/m14260/latest/texturehandout.pdf

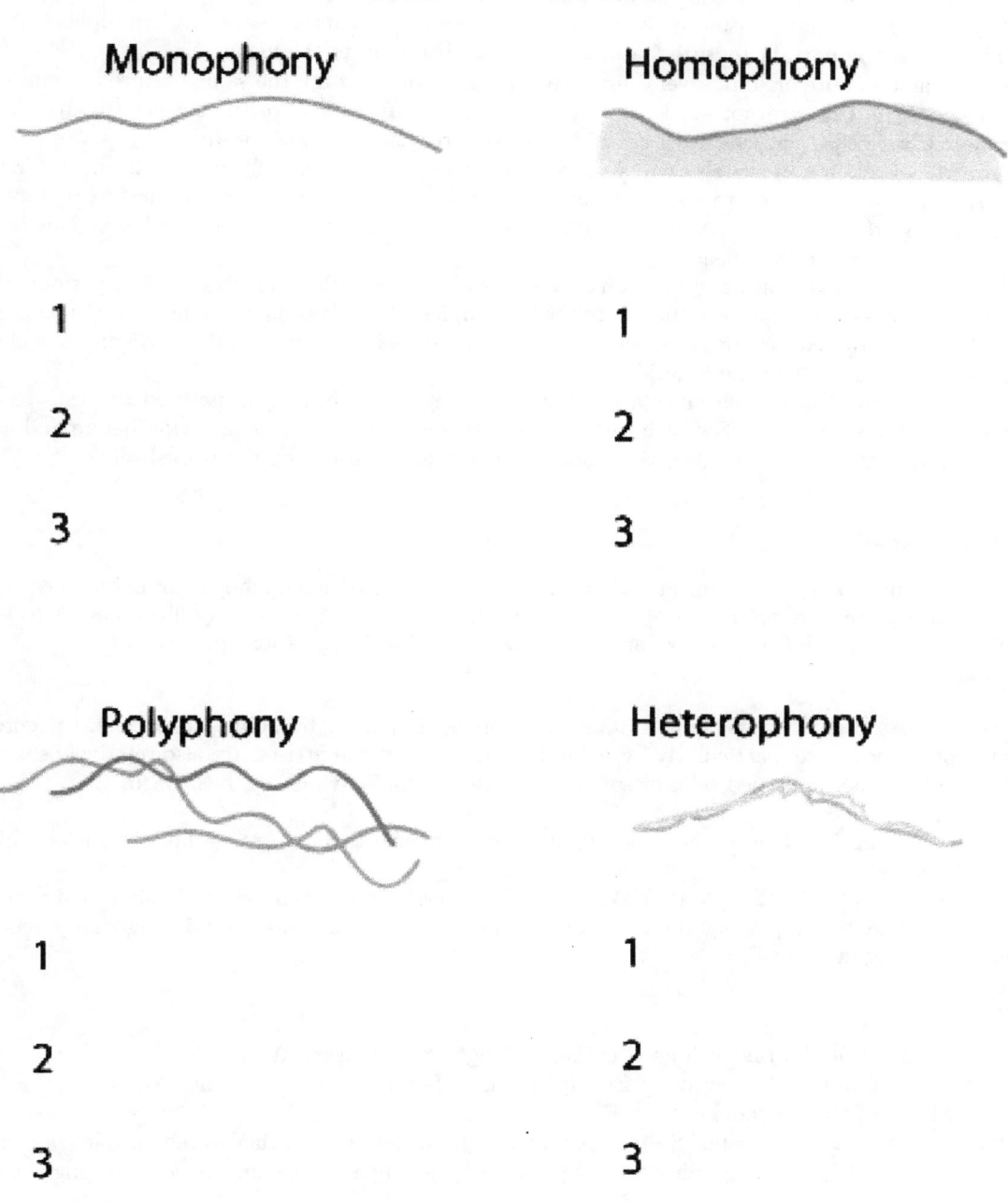

Figure 3.1

Procedure

1. Give out the handouts or write the terms on the board.
2. Give the students the definition of one of the terms and then play two or three examples of it. You may want to introduce the terms in the following order: monophony, homophony, polyphony, heterophony. (Since it is somewhat unusual in Western music[10], you may want to leave out heterophony.)
3. Point out the important texture features as you are listening to the music.
4. Next, play a minute or so of several more recordings, some that are the same texture as your examples and and some that are not. Ask your students to identify which are the correct texture. They can answer when called on, vote with raised hands, or write their answers down.
5. Once they have one texture down, you can introduce a new one. Follow steps 2 and 3 for the new texture, but when you get to step four, see if they can identify which pieces are the first texture studied and which are the second. You can repeat this step for all four textures, until they can accurately identify any texture they hear.
6. If many of your examples and "mystery" selections are from other cultures or time periods, you may want to discuss this when you introduce your examples. Then you may also ask the students to make a guess as to the culture or time period of your "mystery" selections, and ask them what elements - including texture - help them decide.
7. If you are using the worksheet as a handout, you may also use it as a final texture test. Play a few more selections for them. For each selection, tell them the name of the selection before and after you play it, and let them write down the name in the correct category on the worksheet.

3.2.1 Suggested Music

There are, of course, many recordings that are excellent examples of homophony or of polyphony, but many great works change texture often, in order to be more interesting. Monophony is a little harder to find, and heterophony even more difficult. Below are just a few easy-to-find suggestions in each category.

Monophony

- Here is an excerpt[11] from James Romig's[12] Sonnet 2, played by John McMurtery. Recordings of unaccompanied flute, particularly by Asian or Native American artists, are also relatively easy to find.
- A suite for unaccompanied cello or sonata for unaccompanied violin by J. S. Bach.
- Gregorian chant
- Sing something for them without accompaniment, or have them sing together the melody of a song they all know.
- Long sections of "The People that Walked in Darkness" aria in Handel's "Messiah" are monophonic (the instruments are playing the same line as the voice). Apparently Handel associates monophony with "walking in darkness"!

Homophony

- A classic Scott Joplin rag such as "Peacherine Rag" or "The Easy Winners"
- The "graduation march" section of Edward Elgar's "Pomp and Circumstance No. 1"
- The "March of the Toreadors" from Bizet's *Carmen*
- No. 1 ("Granada") of Albeniz' Suite Española for guitar, and many other works for solo classical guitar
- If the students have been learning a vocal piece with melody and harmony, have them sing it with both parts
- The latest hit tune by a major pop solo vocalist
- A well-known choir singing a hymn or Christmas tune
- The opening section of the "Overture" Of Handel's "Messiah" (The second section of the overture is polyphonic)

---

[10]"What Kind of Music is That?" <http://cnx.org/content/m11421/latest/>
[11]http://cnx.org/content/m14260/latest/sonnet2exc.mp3
[12]http://www.jamesromig.com

- Most Indian Classical music is homophonic.

Polyphony

- Pachelbel's Canon
- Anything titled "fugue", "invention", "round", or "canon"
- Have the students sing a round they know, in at least two parts
- The final "Amen" chorus of Handel's "Messiah"; many of the choruses of the messiah move back and forth between homophony and polyphony.
- The trio strain of Sousa's "Stars and Stripes Forever", with the famous piccolo countermelody
- The "One Day More" chorus from the musical "Les Miserables"
- The first movement of Holst's 1st Suite for Military Band

Heterophony

- There is some heterophony (with some instruments playing more ornaments than others) in "Donulmez Aksamin" and in "Urfaliyim Ezelden" on the Turkish Music[13] page.
- The performance of "Lonesome Valley" by the Fairfield Four on the "O Brother, Where Art Thou" soundtrack is quite heterophonic. (Old-style blues owes more to African than to Western traditions.)
- This texture is also common in the Bluegrass, "mountain music", Cajun, and Zydeco traditions. Look for tunes in which the melody is being played by more than one instrument (say fiddle and banjo) at the same time, with each adding its own ornaments and flourishes
- If the students all know a pop tune but have not been rehearsing it together, ask them to sing it together. The result is very likely to be a good example of heterophony.
- Indonesian *gamelan* music is often heterophonic, with different kinds of instruments playing different versions of the same melody at the same time, but it can be difficult for someone unaccustomed to this style of music to hear that that is what is happening. If you use some *gamelan* examples, make sure the heterophony is clearly audible.
- If anyone knows of any other good links or easy-to-find recordings of heterophony, or can share an audio file of a good example, please contact me.

3.3 An Introduction to Counterpoint[14]

3.3.1 Introduction

Counterpoint is an important element of music, but it is not one of the basic elements. Many pieces of music have rhythm (Section 1.1), melody (Section 2.2.1), harmony (Section 2.3.1), color (Section 2.1.1), and texture (Section 3.1), but no real counterpoint. In fact, when describing the texture of a piece of music, two of the most important questions that need to be addressed are: is there counterpoint, and how important is it?

When there is **more than one independent melodic line happening at the same time** in a piece of music, we say that the music is **contrapuntal**. The independent melodic lines are called **counterpoint**. The music that is made up of counterpoint can also be called **polyphony**, or one can say that the music is **polyphonic** or speak of the **polyphonic texture** of the music. Traditionally, vocal music is more likely to be described as **polyphony** and instrumental music is more likely to be described as **counterpoint**. But all of these terms refer to two or more independent, simultaneous melodies. "Simultaneous" means the melodies are happening at the same time. "Independent" means that at any given moment what is happening in one melody (both in the rhythms (Section 1.1) and in the pitches[15]) is probably not the same thing that is happening in the other melody.

---

[13] http://www.focusmm.com/turkey/tr_musmn.htm
[14] This content is available online at <http://cnx.org/content/m11634/1.5/>.
[15] "Pitch: Sharp, Flat, and Natural Notes" <http://cnx.org/content/m10943/latest/>

First, some examples of music that is **not** counterpoint. Obviously, there is no counterpoint if there is no melody at all. If there is one melodic line accompanied only by rhythm, or drones, or only by chords, there is no counterpoint.

Even if different people are singing or playing different parts, it is not necessarily considered counterpoint if the parts are not independent enough, or if one of the parts is very clearly a dominating melody. Many traditional choral pieces are a good example of this. There are four very different singing parts (soprano, alto, tenor, and bass), and each part, sung alone, can seem like its own melody, a melody that does not sound at all like the melody of the piece. But the parts have basically the same rhythms, so that the effect, when sung together, is of chords being sung. "Barbershop"-style music is another good example of this homophonic (Section 3.1.2.2: Homophonic), or chordal, kind of texture, which is not considered counterpoint.

Now for some familiar examples of counterpoint. One of the simplest and most familiar types of counterpoint is the round. In a **round**, everyone sings the same melody, but they start singing it at different times. Although everyone is singing exactly the same tune, at any particular time different people will be singing different parts of it, so the final effect is of independent parts. You may also have heard some Bach fugues or inventions; there are no better examples of counterpoint than these. Another example that may be familiar is the soloist in a pop or gospel song who, after the refrain has been repeated a few times, takes off on a countermelody or descant (p. 72) part while everyone else continues to sing the refrain. The melody instruments in a dixieland band are also generally playing independent parts, giving this genre its "busy" sound. In fact, when music sounds very "busy" or "complex" or when there is so much going on that it gets difficult to decide where the melody is or what part to sing along with, it is likely that you are hearing counterpoint.

Although there is plenty of music that has no counterpoint, independent parts are one of the most basic ways to make music sound rich and interesting. Even if a piece of music cannot really be called "counterpoint" or "polyphony", because it clearly has one melody, the accompaniment (Accompaniment, p. 54) lines may still be quite contrapuntal. Even music that most people would describe as homophonic (Section 3.1.2.2: Homophonic) or chordal (Chords, p. 53), because all the lines have exactly the same rhythm, is often written following the voice-leading rules of counterpoint. This gives the music a much richer, more interesting texture (Section 3.1). Next time you are listening to your favorite song or your favorite piece of music, don't hum along with the melody. Instead, listen to the bass line. Listen to the harmonies (Section 2.3.1), the inner voices (Accompaniment, p. 54) and the instrumental accompaniment parts. Chances are that you will hear some interesting lines, even little pieces of melody, that are completely different from the part you normally hear.

3.3.2 Some Useful Terms

- **Canon** - In a canon, different voices (or instruments) sing (or play) the same melody, with no changes, but at different times. The melody is usually sung at the same pitch or an octave[16] higher or lower, but there are also canons in which the second part sings or plays the melody a perfect fourth or fifth[17] higher or lower than the first part.
- **Round** - In a canon, obviously every section of the canon must "fit" with the section that comes after it. (In other words, they must sound good when sung or played at the same time). A round is a special type of canon in which the last section also fits with the first section, so that the canon can be repeated over and over without stopping. Rounds are usually pretty short and always start at the same note, or the octave.
- **Fugue** - A fugue usually has at least three independent parts, or **voices**. The different voices enter at different times on the same melodic theme (called the **subject**), so that the beginning may sound like a canon. But then the different voices develop the theme in different directions. A second melodic theme (called the **countersubject**) is usually introduced, and the middle of the fugue gets quite intricate, with the subject and countersubject popping in and out of various voices, sometimes in surprising ways

---

[16]"Octaves and the Major-Minor Tonal System" <http://cnx.org/content/m10862/latest/>
[17]"Interval" <http://cnx.org/content/m10867/latest/#p21b>

(upside-down, for example).

- **Countermelody or descant** - Sometimes a piece of music that is basically melody-with-accompaniment (homophonic) will include a single part that is truly independent of the melody. For example, a choral piece might be chordal for a few verses and then, to keep the music interesting and fresh, add an independent part for a flute or for the highest sopranos on the third verse. This is a countermelody, sometimes called a descant part. Gospel and pop singers often add countermelodies, sometimes imrovised, and classical music also contains many, many examples of countermelodies.

3.4 Counterpoint Activities[18]

3.4.1 Introduction

Here are lesson plans for a listening/discussion activity, (Listening For Counterpoint (Section 3.4.2: Listening for Counterpoint)) and two singing activities (Rounds (Section 3.4.3: Rounds) and Countermelodies (Section 3.4.4: Countermelodies)) designed to introduce children to the musical element called counterpoint (Section 3.3). The activities may be used together or separately.

Goals and Requirements

- **Goals** - The student will understand the appropriate musical terms and concepts regarding counterpoint (Section 3.3), be able to identify them when heard in music, and participate in singing that contains counterpoint.
- **Grade Level** - preK-12 (adaptable)
- **Teacher Expertise** - Teacher training in music education is not necessary to present these activities. The teacher should be familiar and comfortable with the terms and concepts regarding counterpoint (Section 3.3). To lead the singing activities, the teacher should be able to sing each part independently and with confidence.
- **Follow-up** - Continue throughout the rest of the school year to introduce music with counterpoint for the students to listen to and perform.

3.4.2 Listening for Counterpoint

Objectives and Assessment

- **Objectives** - While listening to recordings of a variety of music, the student will accurately assess whether each example is contrapuntal or not.
- **Music Standards Addressed** - National Standards for Music Education[19] standard 6 (listening to, analyzing, and describing music).
- **Student Prerequisites** - When listening to music, the students should be able to recognize the melody.
- **Time Requirements** - 20-40 minutes, depending on the number of terms introduced and the number and length of examples.
- **Extensions** - For younger students or students unfamiliar with Classical music, choose short, simple, and very clear examples. older or more musically advanced students, you may choose longer and more complex examples. For more of a challenge, you may also to introduce the concepts of rounds (Section 3.3.2: Some Useful Terms), canons (Section 3.3.2: Some Useful Terms), and/or fugues (Section 3.3.2: Some Useful Terms), and ask the students to decide which of the counterpoint examples fall into these categories.

---

[18] This content is available online at <http://cnx.org/content/m14261/1.4/>.
[19] http://menc.org/resources/view/national-standards-for-music-education

- **Evaluation** - Assess students on active participation in the discussion and on accurate use of the terms and correct identification of examples.

Materials and Preparation

- You will need a CD or tape player
- Gather the musical examples to play. Know the track numbers or have the tapes ready to play at the right spot.

Suggestions: Contrapuntal Music

- Pachelbel's Canon
- Any piece of music titled "Fugue", "Invention", "Canon", or "Round"
- Much (but not all!) of J. S. Bach's music.
- Handel's "Messiah" has many examples both of music that is contrapuntal and music that is not contrapuntal.
- Dixieland jazz
- Many of J. P Sousa's marches have very audible counterpoint, in the low brass for example, or in the piccolo part of "stars and Stripes Forever".

Suggestions: Music that is not Contrapuntal

- Most hymns and carols
- Most barbershop music
- Most classic ragtime (Scott Joplin's rags, for example), and most swing-era jazz
- Most music for an unaccompanied classical guitar, for one unaccompanied bagpipes or accordion, for an unaccompanied singer or string, woodwind, or brass player
- plainchant (Gregorian chant, for example)
- Most popular music and folk music
- Most of the classical music of India

Procedure

1. Play a couple of your chosen non-counterpoint examples. Point out that there is only one melody. See if they can sing along with it.
2. Introduce the terms that you wish the students to learn; these terms may include **counterpoint**, **contrapuntal**, **polyphony**, **polyphonic**, **round**, **canon**, **fugue** or **countermelody**. (See Introduction to Counterpoint (Section 3.3).)
3. Play a couple of your chosen conterpoint examples. Ask them if they can hear more than one melody at the same time. Point out the different voices as best you can; if they are entering one at a time, as in Pachelbel's Canon, point out the entrances. If the parts are singable, can you or they sing along with the melodies of the different parts? If you are introducing these terms, point out which of your examples are rounds/canons (completely imitative), fugues (partly imitative), or non-imitative counterpoint.
4. Now play the rest of your examples and ask them to identify whether each is contrapuntal or not. If the class has discussed rounds, canons, fugues, and countermelodies, can they identify any of these in the examples?

3.4.3 Rounds

Objectives and Assessment

- **Objectives** - The students will learn the melody of a round and sing it, first all together as a single group, and then broken into smaller groups, with each group singing one part of the round.
- **Music Standards Addressed** - National Standards for Music Education[20] standard 1 (singing, alone

---

[20] http://menc.org/resources/view/national-standards-for-music-education

and with others, a varied repertoire of music).
- **Student Prerequisites** - The student should be able to sing a tune, as part of a group, with accurate pitch and rhythm.
- **Time Requirements** - If the students are learning a new tune, this will work best if spread over several short (5-15-minute) sessions over the period of a week or two. Early sessions should concentrate on learning the tune and singing it with confidence. Introduce and practice the round aspect only after the students know the song well. The number of sessions will depend on the students' ability and experience, and the length and difficulty of the music.
- **Evaluation** - Assess students on active participation in the singing and ability to remain on their part when other parts are introduced.

Materials and Preparation

- Choose the round(s) to be taught. For very young students, it's hard to beat the old stand-by's like "Row, Row, Row your Boat", "Three Blind Mice", and "Frere Jaque". For older students, there will be some rounds to choose from in almost any children's sing-along book (for example, those published by your church or scouting organization, or the "Sing Along" book in the "Wee Sing" series). Or you may use the rounds below. "Hey Ho" is easy enough for even young children; "Dona Nobis Pacem" is challenging enough to be interesting to older students.
- Have copies for the students of the words only, or of the words and music, if you think they are needed.
- If you will be uncomfortable singing or playing the melody by yourself, have a tape (and player) for the students to listen to and sing along with. If at all possible, find a version that includes the melody in unison (everyone singing all together without the round). You can listen to the melody of Hey Ho[21] or Dona Nobis Pacem[22] here.

---

[21] http://cnx.org/content/m14261/latest/HeyHo.mid
[22] http://cnx.org/content/m14261/latest/DonaNobis.mid

(a) Hey Ho

(b) Dona Nobis Pacem

Figure 3.2

Procedure

1. Ask the students if they know what a round is. Let them explain how a round works if they can; if not, you explain. (See Counterpoint for Everyone (Section 3.3.2: Some Useful Terms).)
2. If appropriate, introduce the term **counterpoint** and/or **canon**. Explain that in counterpoint, there is more than one melody happening at the same time. Tell your students that a round (or canon) is a special type of counterpoint: all the melodies are actually the same, but since they start at different times, at any particular time they sound different.
3. Sing or play your chosen round for the students.
4. Sing or play the round repeatedly, asking the students to join in with you as soon as they can. Sing it all together as many times as necessary until everyone can sing the melody confidently. For very young students, this may take more than one session.
5. Once everyone is very comfortable with the melody, try breaking into two groups and singing the song as a round. Group 2 starts singing at the beginning when Group 1 reaches the "2" marked in the music. If that goes well, you can try breaking into more groups. Group 3 starts singing at the beginning when Group 1 reaches the "3" marked in the music.

3.4.4 Countermelodies

Objectives and Assessment

- **Objectives** - As a group, the students will learn the melody or countermelody of a song, and will sing their part while another group sings the other part.

- **Music Standards Addressed** - National Standards for Music Education[23] standard 1 (singing, alone and with others, a varied repertoire of music).
- **Student Prerequisites** - The student should be able to sing a tune, as part of a group, with accurate pitch and rhythm.
- **Time Requirements** - If the students are learning a new tune, this will work best if spread over several short (5-15-minute) sessions over the period of a week or two. Early sessions should concentrate on learning the parts and singing them with confidence. Try putting them together only after the students know both parts well. The number of sessions will depend on the students' ability and experience, and the length and difficulty of the music.
- **Evaluation** - Assess students on active participation in the singing and ability to remain on their part when other parts are introduced.
- **Adaptations and Extensions** - Ask younger, musically inexperienced students to learn very simple, repetitive, countermelodies. Ask advanced or gifted students to learn and be able to do either part as required.

Materials and Preparation

- Choose the song to be taught. Songs with countermelodies can be a little harder to find than rounds. You are basically looking for a song that has two **independent** parts (not just a harmony) to be sung at the same time. They may have the same words, but often do not. If you cannot find a song with a countermelody, you can use the Israeli folk song included here.
- If appropriate, have copies of the words or of the words and music, for the students.
- Be prepared to sing or play both the melody and the countermelody. If you are uncomfortable with this, perhaps you can find (or have someone make) a tape to use instead. The students will need to hear each part separately. Here are the chant melody[24], the verse melody[25], and both together[26] for "Zum Gali Gali".

---

[23] http://menc.org/resources/view/national-standards-for-music-education
[24] http://cnx.org/content/m14261/latest/zggchant.mid
[25] http://cnx.org/content/m14261/latest/zggverse.mid
[26] http://cnx.org/content/m14261/latest/zggboth.mid

Zum Gali Gali

Chant:

Zum ga-li ga-li ga-li, zum ga-li ga- li.

Verses:

1. He- cha- lutz le 'man a- vo- dah
2. Ha- sha- lom le 'man ha 'a- mim

1. A- vo- dah le 'man he- sha- lutz.
2. Ha 'a- mim le 'man ha- sha- lom.

Figure 3.3: You may wish to start the chant before the verses, have some measures of chant between the verses, and end with just chant; but of course the **countermelody** happens when you sing the chant at the same time as the verse.

Procedure

1. If you are teaching terms to your students, explain that countermelodies are also counterpoint. But they are different from rounds because the countermelody is not the same as the melody. It is a completely different tune sung at the same time.
2. Choose a group of students to learn the melody and a group to learn the countermelody. This often works best if the students singing the countermelody are fewer in number but are the more confident singers.
3. Let each group hear their part separately, and let them practice separately, also. If everyone is present for the entire rehearsal, you can encourage them to learn each other's parts so they don't get bored.
4. When both groups are confident with their parts, have them sing together.

3.5 Form in Music[27]

3.5.1 Form is the Basic Structure

Every piece of music has an overall plan or structure, the "big picture", so to speak. This is called the **form** of the music.

It is easy to recognize and grasp the form of some things, because they are small and simple, like a grain of salt, or repetitive, like a wall made of bricks of the same size. Other forms are easy to understand because they are so familiar; if you see dogs more often than you do sea cucumbers, it should be easier for you to recognize the form of an unfamiliar dog than of an unfamiliar sea cucumber. Other things, like a forest ecosystem, or the structure of a government, are so complex that they have to be explored or studied before their structure can be understood.

Musical forms offer a great range of complexity. Most listeners will quickly grasp the form of a short and simple piece, or of one built from many short repetitions. It is also easier to recognize familiar musical forms. The average American, for example, can distinguish easily between the verses and refrain of any pop song, but will have trouble recognizing what is going on in a piece of music for Balinese gamelan. Classical music traditions around the world tend to encourage longer, more complex forms which may be difficult to recognize without the familiarity that comes from study or repeated hearings.

You can enjoy music without recognizing its form, of course. But understanding the form of a piece helps a musician put together a more credible performance of it. Anyone interested in music theory or history, or in arranging or composing music, must have a firm understanding of form. And being able to "see the big picture" does help the listener enjoy the music even more.

3.5.2 Describing Form

Musicians traditionally have two ways to describe the form of a piece of music. One way involves labelling each large section with a letter. The other way is to simply give a name to a form that is very common.

3.5.2.1 Labelling Form With Letters

Letters can be used to label the form of any piece of music, from the simplest to the most complex. Each major section of the music is labelled with a letter; for example, the first section is the A section. If the second section (or third or fourth) is exactly the same as the first, it is also labelled A. If it is very much like the A section, but with some important differences, it can be labelled A' (pronounced "A prime"). The A' section can also show up later in the piece, or yet another variation of A, A" (pronounced "A double prime") can show up, and so on.

The first major section of the piece that is very different from A is labelled B, and other sections that are like it can be labelled B, B', B", and so on. Sections that are not like A or B are labelled C, and so on.

How do you recognize the sections? With familiar kinds of music, this is pretty easy. (See Figure 3.4 (Some Familiar Forms) for some examples of forms that will be familiar to most listeners.) With unfamiliar types of music, it can be more of a challenge. Whether the music is classical, modern, jazz, or pop, listen for repeated sections of music. Also, listen for big changes, in the rhythm (Section 1.1), melody (Section 2.2.1), harmony (Section 2.3.1), texture (Section 3.1), and timbre (Section 2.1.1). A new section that is not a repetition will usually have noticeable differences in more than one of these areas. For an excellent discussion of form, with plenty of chances to practice hearing the beginnings of new sections, please see Professor Brandt's Sound Reasoning[28] course. In particular, Musical Form[29] deals with recognizing when something new is being introduced (A/B instead of A only), and Time's Effect on the Material[30] deals with recognizing when a section reappears changed (A', B', or A").

---

[27]This content is available online at <http://cnx.org/content/m10842/2.11/>.
[28]*Sound Reasoning* <http://cnx.org/content/col10214/latest/>
[29]"Musical Form" <http://cnx.org/content/m11629/latest/>
[30]"Time's Effect on the Material" <http://cnx.org/content/m11434/latest/>

Some Familiar Forms

Typical Children's Nursery Rhyme:	A	
	One short section with no major changes in the sound of the music	A
Typical Hymn (no refrain):	A A' A"	
First Verse	Everyone sings the melody	A
Second Verse	Choir adds harmonies	A'
Third Verse	Organ adds more complex accompaniment	A"
Typical Pop Song:	A B A' B A" B' OR A B A' B C B'	
First verse	Solo singer with quiet instrumental backup	A
Refrain	Different melody, different chord progression, often a "bigger", more complex texture than verse.	B
Second verse	Different words, but the music is very similar to the first verse (usually with small differences)	A'
Refrain	Same as first refrain (no noticeable differences)	B
Third verse OR Bridge	Same comments as second verse OR New melody with new chord progression	A" OR C
Final Refrain	May add more vocal or instrumental parts, for most complex texture yet	B'

Figure 3.4: Most folk and popular music features simple forms that encourage participation.

Exercise 3.1 *(Solution on p. 87.)*

Practice identifying some easy musical forms. Pick some favorite songs and listen to each repeatedly until you are satisfied that you have identified its full form using letters and primes. Compare the forms of the tunes to spot similarities and differences.

Listen for:

- **Verses** have the same melody but different words.
- **Refrains** have the same melody and the same words.
- **Bridge Sections** are new material that appears late in the song, usually appearing only once or twice, often in place of a verse and usually leading into the refrain. (You may want to note the differences - and the similarity - in the use of the term **bridge** by popular musicians and jazz musicians; see below (Some Common Forms, p. 82)).
- **Instrumentals** are important sections that have no vocals. They can come at the beginning or end, or in between other sections. Is there more than one? Do they have the same melody as a verse or refrain? Are they similar to each other?

While discussing a piece of music in detail, musicians may also use letters to label smaller parts of the piece within larger sections, even down to labelling individual phrases (Section 2.2.1.4: Melodic Phrases). For example, the song "The Girl I Left Behind" has many verses with no refrain, an A A' A"- type form. However, a look (Figure 3.5: Phrase Structure in "The Girl I Left Behind") at the tune of one verse shows that within that overall form is an A A' B A" phrase structure.

Figure 3.5: In detailed discussions of a piece of music, smaller sections, and even individual phrases, may also be labelled with letters, in order to discuss the piece in greater detail. The A A B A form of this verse is very common, found in verses of everything from folk to jazz to pop music. Verses of blues songs are more likely to have an A A' B form.

Exercise 3.2   *(Solution on p. 87.)*

Now try labeling the phrases of a verse or a refrain of some of the songs you listened to in Exercise 3.1. Listen for phrases that use similar melodies. (Sometimes, but not always, they even use the same words.) How many of your refrains and verses were basically A A B A? What were the others?

3.5.2.2 Naming Forms

Often a musical form becomes so popular with composers that it is given a name. For example, if a piece of music is called a "theme and variations", it is expected to have an overall plan quite different from a piece called a "rondo". (Specifically, the theme and variations would follow an A A' A" A'''... plan, with each section being a new variation on the theme in the first section. A rondo follows an A B A C A ... plan, with a familiar section returning in between sections of new music.)

Also, many genres of music tend to follow a preset form, like the "typical pop song form" in Figure 3.4 (Some Familiar Forms). A **symphony**, for example, is usually a piece of music written for a fairly large number of instruments. It is also associated with a particular form, so knowing that a piece of music is called a symphony should lead you to expect certain things about it. For example, listeners familiar with the symphonic form expect a piece called a symphony to have three or four (depending on when it was written) main sections, called **movements**. They expect a moment of silence in between movements, and also expect the movements to sound very different from each other; for example if the first movement is fast and loud, they might expect that the second movement would be slow and quiet. If they have heard many symphonies, they also would not be at all surprised if the first movement is in sonata form and the third movement is based on a dance.

> NOTE: Although a large group of people who play classical music together is often called a symphony, the more accurate term for the group is **orchestra**. The confusion occurs because many orchestras call themselves "symphony orchestras" because they spend so much time playing symphonies (as opposed to, for example, an "opera orchestra" or a "pops orchestra").

Other kinds of music are also so likely to follow a particular overall plan that they have become associated with a particular form. You can hear musicians talk about something being concerto form or sonata form, for example (even if the piece is not technically a concerto or sonata). Particular dances (a minuet, for example), besides having a set tempo (Section 1.5) and time signature[31], will sometimes have a set form that suits the dance steps. And many marches are similar enough in form that there are names for the expected sections (first strain, second strain, trio, break strain).

But it is important to remember that forms are not sets of rules that composers are required to follow. Some symphonies don't have silence between movements, and some don't use the sonata form in any of their movements. Plenty of marches have been written that don't have a trio section, and the development section of a sonata movement can take unexpected turns. And hybrid forms, like the sonata rondo, can become popular with some composers. After all, in architecture, "house" form suggests to most Americans a front and back door, a dining room off the kitchen, and bedrooms with closets, but an architect is free to leave out the dining room, and put the main door at the side of the house and the closets in the bathrooms. Whether a piece of music is a march, a sonata, or a theme and variations, the composer is always free to experiment with the overall architecture of the piece.

Being able to spot that overall architecture as we listen - knowing, so to speak, which room we are in right now - gives us important clues that help us understand and appreciate the music.

Some Common Forms

- **Through-composed** - One section (usually not very long) that does not contain any large repetitions. If a short piece includes repeated phrases, it may be classified by the structure of its phrases.
- **Strophic** - Composed of verses. The music is repeated sections with fairly small changes. May or may not include a refrain (p. 80).
- **Variations** - One section repeated many times. Most commonly, the melody remains recognizable in each section, and the underlying harmonic structure[32] remains basically the same, but big changes in rhythm (Section 1.1), tempo (Section 1.5), texture (Section 3.1), or timbre (Section 2.1.1) keep each section sounding fresh and interesting. Writing a set of variations is considered an excellent exercise for students interested in composing, arranging, and orchestration.

---

[31]"Time Signature" <http://cnx.org/content/m10956/latest/>
[32]"Beginning Harmonic Analysis" <http://cnx.org/content/m11643/latest/>

- **Jazz standard song form** - Jazz utilizes many different forms, but one very common form is closely related to the strophic and variation forms. A chord progression (Chords, p. 53) in A A B A form (with the B section called the bridge (p. 80)) is repeated many times. On the first and last repetition, the melody is played or sung, and soloists improvise during the other repetitions. The overall form of verse-like repetition, with the melody played only the first and final times, and improvisations on the other repetitions, is very common in jazz even when the A A B A song form is not being used.
- **Rondo** - One section returns repeatedly, with a section of new music before each return. (A B A C A ; sometimes A B A C A B A)
- **Dance forms** - Dance forms usually consist of repeated sections (so there is plenty of music to dance to), with each section containing a set number of measures[33] (often four, eight, sixteen, or thirty-two) that fits the dance steps. Some very structured dance forms (Minuet, for example) are associated even with particular phrase (Section 2.2.1.4: Melodic Phrases) structures and harmonic progressions[34] within each section.
- **Binary Form** - Two different main sections (A B). Commonly in Western[35] classical music, the A section will move away from the tonic[36], with a strong cadence[37] in another key, and the B section will move back and end strongly in the tonic.
- **Ternary Form** - Three main sections, usually A B A or A B A'.
- **Cyclic Form** - There are two very different uses of this term. One refers to long multimovement works (a "song cycle", for example) that have an overarching theme and structure binding them together. It may also refer to a single movement or piece of music with a form based on the constant repetition of a single short section. This may be an exact repetition (**ostinato**) in one part of the music (for example, the bass line, or the rhythm section), while development, variation, or new melodies occur in other parts. Or it may be a repetition that gradually changes and evolves. This intense-repetition type of cyclic form is very common in folk musics around the world and often finds its way into classical and popular musics, too.
- **Sonata form** - may also be called sonata-allegro or first-movement form. It is in fact often found in the first movement of a sonata, but it has been an extremely popular form with many well-known composers, and so can be found anywhere from the first movement of a quartet to the final movement of a symphony. In this relatively complex form (too complex to outline here), repetition and development of melodic themes within a framework of expected key changes allow the composer to create a long movement that is unified enough that it makes sense to the listener, but varied enough that it does not get boring.

3.6 Music Form Activities[38]

3.6.1 Introduction

The overall structure of a piece of music is one of its most basic and most revealing aspects. Music majors at the university level study the form of important works in great depth and detail. Yet even young children with little musical experience can begin to grasp the basic principles of form in music. This can be part of a music class, but it can also be related to identifying form in other areas such as math, literature, and the visual arts.

Described below are some activities introducing the concepts of Verses (Section 3.6.2: Activity 1: Verses), Refrains (Section 3.6.3: Activity 2: Refrains), AB Forms (Section 3.6.4: Further Practice With Form), and Form in the Arts. You can find the basic concepts necessary at Form in Music (Section 3.5). The course

---

[33]"Time Signature": Section Beats and Measures <http://cnx.org/content/m10956/latest/#s1>
[34]"Beginning Harmonic Analysis" <http://cnx.org/content/m11643/latest/>
[35]"What Kind of Music is That?" <http://cnx.org/content/m11421/latest/>
[36]"Major Keys and Scales" <http://cnx.org/content/m10851/latest/#p1a>
[37]"Cadence in Music" <http://cnx.org/content/m12402/latest/>
[38]This content is available online at <http://cnx.org/content/m13617/1.4/>.

Sound Reasoning[39] is a good introduction to musical form, and you may also want to adapt some of the exercises in that course for your students.

Goals and Assessment

- **Goals** - The student will learn to identify simple music forms presented aurally.
- **Grade Level** - K-12 (adaptable)
- **Student Prerequisites** - Students should be able to recognize and remember repetitions and large changes in basic elements (texture (Section 3.1), timbre (Section 2.1.1), rhythm (Section 1.1), or melody (Section 2.2.1), for example) as they listen to music. If necessary, simply practice recognizing repeated and new material, before doing these exercises. (The course Sound Reasoning[40] is recommended for this.)
- **Teacher Expertise** - The teacher should be familiar and comfortable with the terms and concepts regarding musical form (Section 3.5), and confident and accurate in recognizing the forms presented.
- **Music Standards Addressed** - National Standards for Music Education[41] music standard 6 (listening to, analyzing, and describing music). If Form in the Arts is included, music standard 8 (understanding relationships between music, the other arts, and disciplines outside the arts) is also addressed.
- **Other Subjects Addressed** - You may use the suggestions in Form in the Arts to design a cross-disciplinary lesson that also addresses **visual arts**, **language arts**, or **mathematics**.
- **Evaluation** - For formal assessment, test the students following these activities by playing music that you have not yet analyzed as a class, and have the students identify on paper: whether each selection includes verses and/or refrains, repeated sections or theme with variations, and/or large AB sections, and how many of each. For testing purposes, keep selections short and similar in form to the selections analyzed in class, and play each selection at least twice.

3.6.2 Activity 1: Verses

Objectives and Extensions

- **Time Requirements** - One (approximately 45-minute) class period
- **Objectives** - The student will listen to or perform several examples of vocal music consisting of either a single main section or multiple verses. The student will identify the form of the music and the beginning of each verse.
- **Extensions** - For older or advanced students, include examples from instrumental music that are also simple A or multiple-A form. The student will listen to examples of instrumental music, recognizing whether the form is a single section or (exact or changed) multiple repeats of a section, and will identify the form of the music using the standard A/B method.

Materials and Preparation

- Decide whether you will use recordings for this activity or have the students sing songs they know. A mixture of both will be very effective. Choose some songs that have only one section (one "verse", so to speak; many nursery rhymes have only one section, as does "Happy Birthday to You".). Also choose some that have more than one verse, but don't include any songs with refrains or choruses in this activity. If you want to stretch the children's listening skills, include some recordings of music that is unfamiliar, but again play only songs with a single section, or verses only, or instrumental music that is only one section or a section with its repeat, so that it sounds like two verses. Marches and dances are a good source of music with repeated sections. If you think your students will be able to hear the "theme" in its new disguise in each variation, a "theme and variations" is also a very good example of a multiple-A-section form.

---

[39] Sound Reasoning <http://cnx.org/content/col10214/latest/>
[40] <http://cnx.org/content/col101214/latest/>
[41] http://menc.org/resources/view/national-standards-for-music-education

- If you are using recordings, you will need a tape or CD player, and some recordings of age-appropriate songs. Use some songs that are familiar to them and some that aren't. Have the tapes ready at the appropriate spot, or know the track numbers on the CD.

Procedure

- Tell your students that the **form** of a piece of music is just a description or list of the main sections of the music. If your students are old enough and experienced enough, you may use the discussion in Form in Music (Section 3.5.2.1: Labelling Form With Letters) to introduce the idea of labelling sections with letters.
- Ask the students if they know what a verse is in music. They may know but have trouble explaining. Ask if they can sing more than one verse of a song. How are the verses different? (Usually the words are different.) How are they the same? (Usually the music is the same.) If they can't answer any questions even with some prompting, explain that each verse of a song has the same melody but different words.
- Play a recorded song with more than one verse, or have the students sing a song they know. Point out to them when each new verse starts.
- Play more recordings, or sing together some more songs, letting the students point out when each new verse starts (they can raise their hands, or clap at the beginning of each verse, for example). Ask them to count the verses of each song, and to identify which songs have only one verse.
- If you include instrumental selections, ask the students to identify similarities and differences between the instrumental and vocal music. Have the students identify the beginning of section repeats, or beginnings of new variations.
- If you are including a discussion of A/B forms, write the forms of the songs on the board as you sing or listen to them. (Verse forms will mostly look something like A or A A A or A A' A"; you can let your students decide which verses are different enough to give primes (p. 79).)

3.6.3 Activity 2: Refrains

Objectives and Extensions

- **Time Requirements** - One (approximately 45-minute) class period
- **Objectives** - The student will listen to or perform several examples of vocal music consisting of verses with a contrasting refrain. The student will identify the form of the music and identify each verse and refrain.
- **Extensions** - For older or advanced students, include examples from instrumental music that are also simple A/B or repeated A/B form. The student will listen to examples of instrumental music, recognizing whether the form is a single section (A), two contrasting sections (AB) or (exact or changed) multiple repeats of a single idea (AA'...), or multiple repeats of two contrasting ideas (ABA'B...), and will identify the form of the music using the standard A/B method.

Materials and Preparation

- The preparation for this activity is about the same as for the previous activity, but this time choose songs that have refrains. It's best to use refrains that are musically very different from the verses (different melody (Section 2.2.1), chord progression (Chords, p. 53), texture (Section 3.1), etc.). It is more difficult to draw parallels between verses and refrains and instrumental music, but you might play for your students some instrumental music that has a section that keeps returning, in between sections that are different from each other, (**rondo** form, for example), discussing the similarities and differences between this and vocal-music refrains.

Procedure

- If is is appropriate, using the discussion in Form in Music (Section 3.5.2.1: Labelling Form With Letters) as an outline, discuss the process of labelling sections of music.
- Ask the students if they know the difference between a verse and a refrain (or chorus) in music. Even if they do know, they may have trouble explaining. Ask if they can give an example or sing the refrain (or chorus) of a song. If they have no idea, even with prompting, tell your students that the words are the same each time you sing a **refrain** or **chorus**, but the words to each verse are usually different.
- Sing together or play a recorded song for them. Let them point out (or point out for them if necessary) when each verse and each refrain starts.
- Continue to sing together or play more songs, letting them identify the verses and refrains, until they can do this with confidence. (You may have to play unfamiliar songs for them more than once.) They can raise one hand during a verse and the other during a refrain, or clap at the beginning of a verse and stomp at the beginning of a refrain, or sit for verses and stand up for refrains.
- Ask your students why they think some songs have refrains? (Everyone can learn the refrain and join in on it.) Why do they have verses? (A song with only refrains would get pretty boring.)
- If the students can do the above easily, you can include a more formal study of musical form. Pick a couple of the songs and put their form on the board with A's and B's. Let the students decide whether the verses and refrains are different enough to get different letters (in some songs, the refrain has the same music as the verses), and whether and when primes need to be used. Do any of the songs have a bridge (p. 80), or a verse that's different enough that a C should be used?

3.6.4 Further Practice With Form

If your students are old enough and experienced enough with music, try stretching their ability to identify form by giving them some unfamiliar music that is not in verse form or verse/refrain form (some classical music for example, or music from another culture), and see if they can identify A, B, and maybe C sections. You may wish to prepare a short lecture and/or handouts on the subject using the information in the course Sound Reasoning[42], or in Form in Music (Section 3.5), or at least remind them that they are listening for big changes in the music to identify the beginning of each main section. You can use the examples in Musical Form[43] or Time's Effect on the Material[44], or find your own examples.

3.6.5 General Discussion of Form in the Arts

If your students are also studying form in some other subject - art, poetry, or stories, for example, or even geometry - include a discussion of how form is the same and different in each subject. Do the poetry forms they are studying have anything that comparable to the verses or refrains of a song? Does a painting or story ever have anything that acts like a refrain or a repeated section? If a song or other piece of music tells a story, how does that affect its form? Does anything about these musical forms resemble geometric forms (in the way that a "round" is like a circle, for example)?

---

[42] *Sound Reasoning* <http://cnx.org/content/col10214/latest/>
[43] "Musical Form" <http://cnx.org/content/m11629/latest/>
[44] "Time's Effect on the Material" <http://cnx.org/content/m11434/latest/>

Solutions to Exercises in Chapter 3

Solution to Exercise 3.1 (p. 80)
Your answers will depend on the songs you choose. Check them with a teacher if you can. (Bring the music so the teacher can listen to it while checking your answers.)

Solution to Exercise 3.2 (p. 81)
If one is available, have a music teacher check your answers.

Index of Keywords and Terms

Keywords are listed by the section with that keyword (page numbers are in parentheses). Keywords do not necessarily appear in the text of the page. They are merely associated with that section. *Ex.* apples, § 1.1 (1) **Terms** are referenced by the page they appear on. *Ex.* apples, 1

A accents, § 1.7(16), 18, § 1.9(21)
accompaniment, 54, § 2.3.3(56), § 2.3.5(60)
activities, § 3.4(73)
activity, § 1.2(2), § 1.8(19), § 2.2.2(37), § 2.2.3(39), § 3.2(67)
allegro, § 1.5(12)
andante, § 1.5(12)
antecedent, 34
arpeggiated, 56
arpeggiated chords, 53
arpeggios, 53
attack, 27

B bar, § 1.1(1)
bass line, 54
beat, § 1.1(1), 1, 1
block chords, 53, 56
borrowed division, 6
bridge, 81
broken, 56

C cadence, § 2.3.1(52), 53
canon, § 3.3(71), § 3.4(73), 74, 76
cell, § 2.2.1(32), 35, 35
cells, 44
chord progression, § 2.3.1(52), 53
chordal, § 2.3.3(56)
chords, § 2.3.1(52), 53, 53, § 2.3.3(56)
chorus, § 3.5(79), § 3.6(83), 86
chromatic, 54
clause, § 2.2.4(42)
color, § 2.1.1(27), 27, 27, § 2.1.2(28)
compose, § 2.2.5(46)
composition, § 2.2.5(46)
compound, 6
conjunct, 32
conjunct motion, 39
consequent, 34
contour, 32
contrapuntal, § 3.1(65), 66, § 3.3(71), 71, 74
countermelody, § 3.4(73), 74, 78
counterpoint, 53, § 3.1(65), 66, § 3.3(71), 71, § 3.4(73), 74, 76
countersubject, 72

D descant, 54
diatonic, 54
disjunct, 32
disjunct motion, 39
dissonance, 54
drone, § 2.3.2(54), 56
drones, § 2.3.1(52), 53
duple, 6
dynamics, § 1.7(16), 16, § 1.8(19), § 1.9(21)

E embellishments, 32
English, § 2.2.4(42)

F figure, § 2.2.1(32), 35, 35
form, § 3.5(79), 79, § 3.6(83), 85
forte, § 1.7(16)
fugue, § 3.3(71), § 3.4(73), 74

G grammar, § 2.2.4(42)
grave, § 1.5(12)

H harmonic rhythm, 53
harmonics, § 2.1.2(28)
harmony, § 2.3.1(52), 52, § 2.3.2(54), § 2.3.3(56), § 2.3.4(58), § 2.3.5(60)
heterophonic, § 3.1(65), 66
heterophony, § 3.1(65), 66, § 3.2(67)
homophonic, § 2.3.1(52), § 2.3.3(56), § 2.3.4(58), § 2.3.5(60), § 3.1(65), 66
homophony, § 2.3.1(52), 53, § 2.3.3(56), § 2.3.4(58), § 2.3.5(60), § 3.1(65), 66, § 3.2(67)
homorhythmic, § 2.3.5(60), 61

I implied harmony, § 2.3.1(52), 52
improvisation, § 2.2.5(46)
improvise, § 2.2.5(46)
inner parts, 54
inner voices, 54
instruments, § 2.1.2(28)

INDEX

L language, § 2.2.5(46)
language arts, § 2.2.4(42)
larghetto, § 1.5(12)
largo, § 1.5(12)
legato, 39
leitmotif, 36
lento, § 1.5(12)
lesson plan, § 1.2(2), § 2.2.2(37), § 2.2.3(39), § 3.2(67), § 3.4(73)

M measure, § 1.1(1)
Measure or bar, 1
melodic, § 2.2.1(32)
melodic contour, § 2.2.3(39)
melodic line, 32, 54
melodic phrase, § 2.2.4(42)
melodic shape, § 2.2.3(39)
melody, § 2.2.1(32), 32, § 2.2.2(37), § 2.2.3(39), § 2.2.4(42)
meter, § 1.3(5), 5, 6, § 1.4(7)
metronome, § 1.5(12), 12, § 1.6(15)
monody, § 3.1(65), 65
monophonic, § 3.1(65), 65
monophony, § 3.1(65), 65, § 3.2(67)
motif, § 2.2.1(32), 35, § 2.2.5(46)
motiv, § 2.2.1(32), 35, § 2.2.5(46)
motive, § 2.2.1(32), 35, 35, § 2.2.5(46)
movements, 82
movie music, § 2.2.5(46)
movie score, § 2.2.5(46)
music, § 1.1(1), § 1.2(2), § 1.3(5), § 1.4(7), § 1.5(12), § 1.6(15), § 1.7(16), § 1.8(19), § 1.9(21), § 2.1.1(27), § 2.1.2(28), § 2.2.1(32), § 2.2.2(37), § 2.2.3(39), § 2.3.1(52), § 2.3.4(58), § 3.1(65), § 3.2(67), § 3.3(71), § 3.4(73), § 3.5(79), § 3.6(83)
musical instruments, § 2.1.1(27)

N national art standard 2, § 2.2.3(39)
national art standard 6, § 2.1.2(28), § 2.2.3(39)
national dance standard 1, § 1.4(7), § 1.6(15), § 2.2.3(39)
national dance standard 2, § 1.4(7), § 2.2.3(39)
national English standard 2, § 2.2.4(42)
national English standard 3, § 2.2.3(39), § 2.2.4(42)
national English standard 6, § 2.2.4(42)
national music standard 1, § 1.6(15), § 1.8(19), § 2.2.2(37), § 2.2.4(42), § 3.4(73)
national music standard 2, § 1.2(2), § 1.6(15), § 2.2.4(42)
national music standard 3, § 2.2.5(46)
national music standard 4, § 2.2.5(46)
national music standard 5, § 1.2(2), § 1.4(7), § 1.9(21)
national music standard 6, § 1.2(2), § 1.4(7), § 1.8(19), § 2.1.2(28), § 2.2.2(37), § 2.2.3(39), § 2.2.4(42), § 2.2.5(46), § 3.2(67), § 3.4(73), § 3.6(83)
national music standard 7, § 2.1.2(28)
national music standard 8, § 2.1.2(28), § 2.2.3(39), § 2.2.4(42), § 3.6(83)
national music standard 9, § 1.2(2), § 2.1.2(28), § 2.2.3(39), § 2.2.5(46), § 3.2(67)

O Off the beat, 1
On the beat, 1
on the downbeat, 1
opera, § 2.2.5(46)
orchestra, 82
ornaments, 32
ostinato, 83

P parallel, § 2.3.4(58), 59
parallel harmony, 53, 59
percussion, § 1.2(2)
phrase, § 2.2.1(32), 33, § 2.2.4(42)
piano, § 1.7(16)
polyphonic, § 3.1(65), 66, § 3.3(71), 71, 74
polyphonic texture, 71
polyphony, 53, § 3.1(65), 66, § 3.2(67), § 3.3(71), 71, 71, 74
presto, § 1.5(12)

Q quadruple, 6

R refrain, § 3.5(79), § 3.6(83), 86
rhythm, § 1.1(1), 1, § 1.2(2), § 1.3(5), § 1.4(7), § 1.5(12), § 1.9(21)
rhythm section, § 1.1(1), 2
rondo, 85
round, 72, § 3.4(73), 74
rounds, § 3.3(71)

S scalar, 32
sentence, § 2.2.4(42)
shape, 32
simple, 6
staccato, 39
step-wise, 32
strophe, § 3.6(83)
subject, § 2.2.1(32), 36, 72
symphony, § 3.5(79), 82
Syncopation, 2

T tempo, § 1.5(12), 12, § 1.6(15)
texture, § 3.1(65), 65, § 3.2(67)
theme, § 2.2.1(32), 36, § 2.2.5(46)
themes, 37
timbre, § 2.1.1(27), 27, 27, § 2.1.2(28), 28, 30
time signature, § 1.3(5), § 1.4(7), § 1.5(12)
tone, 27
tone quality, 27
triple, 6

U upbeat, 1

V verse, § 3.5(79), § 3.6(83)
vivace, § 1.5(12)
voices, 72

Attributions

Collection: *The Basic Elements of Music*
Edited by: Catherine Schmidt-Jones
URL: http://cnx.org/content/col10218/1.7/
License: http://creativecommons.org/licenses/by/1.0

Module: "Rhythm"
By: Catherine Schmidt-Jones
URL: http://cnx.org/content/m11646/1.4/
Pages: 1-2
Copyright: Catherine Schmidt-Jones
License: http://creativecommons.org/licenses/by/1.0

Module: "Simple Rhythm Activities"
By: Catherine Schmidt-Jones
URL: http://cnx.org/content/m14258/1.6/
Pages: 2-5
Copyright: Catherine Schmidt-Jones
License: http://creativecommons.org/licenses/by/2.0/

Module: "Meter in Music"
By: Catherine Schmidt-Jones
URL: http://cnx.org/content/m12405/1.7/
Pages: 5-7
Copyright: Catherine Schmidt-Jones
License: http://creativecommons.org/licenses/by/1.0

Module: "Musical Meter Activities"
By: Catherine Schmidt-Jones
URL: http://cnx.org/content/m13616/1.5/
Pages: 7-12
Copyright: Catherine Schmidt-Jones
License: http://creativecommons.org/licenses/by/2.0/

Module: "Tempo"
By: Catherine Schmidt-Jones
URL: http://cnx.org/content/m11648/1.6/
Pages: 12-14
Copyright: Catherine Schmidt-Jones
License: http://creativecommons.org/licenses/by/1.0

Module: "A Tempo Activity"
By: Catherine Schmidt-Jones
URL: http://cnx.org/content/m14180/1.5/
Pages: 15-16
Copyright: Catherine Schmidt-Jones
License: http://creativecommons.org/licenses/by/2.0/

Module: "Dynamics and Accents in Music"
By: Catherine Schmidt-Jones
URL: http://cnx.org/content/m11649/1.7/
Pages: 16-19
Copyright: Catherine Schmidt-Jones
License: http://creativecommons.org/licenses/by/1.0

Module: "A Musical Dynamics Activity"
By: Catherine Schmidt-Jones
URL: http://cnx.org/content/m13463/1.5/
Pages: 19-21
Copyright: Catherine Schmidt-Jones
License: http://creativecommons.org/licenses/by/2.0/

Module: "A Musical Accent Activity"
By: Catherine Schmidt-Jones
URL: http://cnx.org/content/m13462/1.6/
Pages: 21-24
Copyright: Catherine Schmidt-Jones
License: http://creativecommons.org/licenses/by/2.0/

Module: "Timbre: The Color of Music"
By: Catherine Schmidt-Jones
URL: http://cnx.org/content/m11059/2.8/
Pages: 27-28
Copyright: Catherine Schmidt-Jones
License: http://creativecommons.org/licenses/by/1.0

Module: "Timbre Activities"
By: Catherine Schmidt-Jones
URL: http://cnx.org/content/m14259/1.3/
Pages: 28-31
Copyright: Catherine Schmidt-Jones
License: http://creativecommons.org/licenses/by/2.0/

Module: "Melody"
By: Catherine Schmidt-Jones
URL: http://cnx.org/content/m11647/1.7/
Pages: 32-37
Copyright: Catherine Schmidt-Jones
License: http://creativecommons.org/licenses/by/1.0

Module: "A Melody Activity"
By: Catherine Schmidt-Jones
URL: http://cnx.org/content/m11833/1.7/
Pages: 37-39
Copyright: Catherine Schmidt-Jones
License: http://creativecommons.org/licenses/by/1.0

Module: "The Shape of a Melody"
By: Catherine Schmidt-Jones
URL: http://cnx.org/content/m11832/1.4/
Pages: 39-42
Copyright: Catherine Schmidt-Jones
License: http://creativecommons.org/licenses/by/1.0

ATTRIBUTIONS

Module: "Melodic Phrases"
By: Catherine Schmidt-Jones
URL: http://cnx.org/content/m11879/1.4/
Pages: 42-46
Copyright: Catherine Schmidt-Jones
License: http://creativecommons.org/licenses/by/1.0

Module: "Theme and Motif in Music"
By: Catherine Schmidt-Jones
URL: http://cnx.org/content/m11880/1.4/
Pages: 46-52
Copyright: Catherine Schmidt-Jones
License: http://creativecommons.org/licenses/by/1.0

Module: "Harmony"
By: Catherine Schmidt-Jones
URL: http://cnx.org/content/m11654/1.7/
Pages: 52-54
Copyright: Catherine Schmidt-Jones
License: http://creativecommons.org/licenses/by/1.0

Module: "Harmony with Drones"
By: Catherine Schmidt-Jones
URL: http://cnx.org/content/m11844/1.1/
Pages: 54-56
Copyright: Catherine Schmidt-Jones
License: http://creativecommons.org/licenses/by/1.0

Module: "Simple Chordal Harmony"
By: Catherine Schmidt-Jones
URL: http://cnx.org/content/m11875/1.2/
Pages: 56-58
Copyright: Catherine Schmidt-Jones
License: http://creativecommons.org/licenses/by/1.0

Module: "Parallel Harmonies"
By: Catherine Schmidt-Jones
URL: http://cnx.org/content/m11878/1.1/
Pages: 58-60
Copyright: Catherine Schmidt-Jones
License: http://creativecommons.org/licenses/by/1.0

Module: "Independent Harmonies"
By: Catherine Schmidt-Jones
URL: http://cnx.org/content/m11874/1.2/
Pages: 60-63
Copyright: Catherine Schmidt-Jones
License: http://creativecommons.org/licenses/by/1.0

Module: "The Textures of Music"
By: Catherine Schmidt-Jones
URL: http://cnx.org/content/m11645/1.7/
Pages: 65-67
Copyright: Catherine Schmidt-Jones
License: http://creativecommons.org/licenses/by/1.0

Module: "A Musical Textures Activity"
By: Catherine Schmidt-Jones
URL: http://cnx.org/content/m14260/1.4/
Pages: 67-71
Copyright: Catherine Schmidt-Jones
License: http://creativecommons.org/licenses/by/2.0/

Module: "An Introduction to Counterpoint"
By: Catherine Schmidt-Jones
URL: http://cnx.org/content/m11634/1.5/
Pages: 71-73
Copyright: Catherine Schmidt-Jones
License: http://creativecommons.org/licenses/by/1.0

Module: "Counterpoint Activities"
By: Catherine Schmidt-Jones
URL: http://cnx.org/content/m14261/1.4/
Pages: 73-78
Copyright: Catherine Schmidt-Jones
License: http://creativecommons.org/licenses/by/2.0/

Module: "Form in Music"
By: Catherine Schmidt-Jones
URL: http://cnx.org/content/m10842/2.11/
Pages: 79-83
Copyright: Catherine Schmidt-Jones
License: http://creativecommons.org/licenses/by/1.0

Module: "Music Form Activities"
By: Catherine Schmidt-Jones
URL: http://cnx.org/content/m13617/1.4/
Pages: 83-86
Copyright: Catherine Schmidt-Jones
License: http://creativecommons.org/licenses/by/2.0/

The Basic Elements of Music

Explanations (suitable for any age) of the basic elements of music, with suggested activities for introducing the each concept to children at early elementary school level. The course may be used by instructors not trained in music; all necessary definitions and explanations are included.

About Connexions

Since 1999, Connexions has been pioneering a global system where anyone can create course materials and make them fully accessible and easily reusable free of charge. We are a Web-based authoring, teaching and learning environment open to anyone interested in education, including students, teachers, professors and lifelong learners. We connect ideas and facilitate educational communities.

Connexions's modular, interactive courses are in use worldwide by universities, community colleges, K-12 schools, distance learners, and lifelong learners. Connexions materials are in many languages, including English, Spanish, Chinese, Japanese, Italian, Vietnamese, French, Portuguese, and Thai. Connexions is part of an exciting new information distribution system that allows for **Print on Demand Books**. Connexions has partnered with innovative on-demand publisher QOOP to accelerate the delivery of printed course materials and textbooks into classrooms worldwide at lower prices than traditional academic publishers.